To Beck,
Happy
with

LIVING

HOPE

A Collection for Holy Week and Easter

Andy March

Halwill Publishing

First published in Great Britain in 2023 by Halwill Publishing,
99 Buckingham Rise, Coventry CV5 9HF

For permission to publish, distribute or otherwise reproduce this work, please contact the author at info@halwillpublishing.co.uk.

ISBN 978-1-7398051-2-8

A CIP catalogue record for this book is available from the British Library.

All scripture quotations are from the Holy Bible, New International Version® Anglicized, NIV® Copyright © 1979, 1984, 2011 by Biblica, Inc.® Used by permission. All rights reserved worldwide.

Cover design: Andy March

Contents

Part 3 – Proclaiming Hope – the message of Holy Week and Easter

Part 4 – Easter for All Ages

Part 5 – Responding to Hope

Part 6 – Journeying in Hope

Introduction

As a fulltime church leader, I have possibly the best job in the world. Why? Because I get to tell people about Jesus. I love Jesus. Thanks to my parents I have always known Jesus as part of my life and sought to follow him. One of the great privileges of being a vicar is that I get to lead my church through the yearly celebration of Holy Week and Easter. What a rollercoaster it is! We journey together from the highs of Palm Sunday through to the mystery of the Last Supper, the despair and darkness of Good Friday and finally, the joy and hope of Resurrection Day. While it's a massive privilege to preach and teach at this time, there's also a challenge – how can I keep it fresh and relevant to my church community? How can I ensure that together we, in the words of Matt Redman, "lose the wonder of your mercy"[*]?

I will never forget, in my first year as a curate (an assistant vicar), being tasked by my training incumbent with leading the "Last Hour" service for Good Friday. For those non-Anglicans out there, this is a service of reflection, worship and prayer that normally takes place at 2pm, so that they end at the time Jesus took his last breath (for two days, at least!). The only problem was that, not being a very good Anglican, I had never actually been to a "Last Hour" service; I wasn't altogether sure what one of these was – I guessed there would be hymns, prayers and readings from one of the Passion Narratives. But what else? How on earth would I fill the time? I looked for inspiration online, but with no luck. So, with increasing desperation, I sat and prayed, read the Bible, and started to think; what if I put myself in the shoes of the characters portrayed so vividly and masterfully by the Gospel writers and imagined their thoughts, motivations and feelings

[*] "Wonder", performed by Matt Redman on *Your Grace Finds Me* (2013) and written by Jonas Myrin and Matt Redman

9

at this most momentous time in history? Could God speak to us through this somehow? I felt most inspired by John's Gospel, so used that as the Scriptural basis for "Faith, hope and courage – a devotional service" (see page 81). I didn't know if this was what I was supposed to do with this service, so I was greatly encouraged by the positive comments I received from those who attended. I must have done something right!

That "Last Hour" service was a *Kairos** moment for me; it marked the moment that I discovered I could use another lifelong passion I've had – a passion for telling stories – for God's purposes, and in my day-to-day ministry. Since then, I've had such joy in finding ways for these timeless and ancient truths to hit home today, whether for my regular congregation, a hall full of schoolchildren, an all-age congregation, or occasional visitors to church. If I can find a different way to convey essential truths, I will, even if it involves looking silly (which it often has, as I've dressed up as a Roman centurion, a first century disciple, complete with fake beard, and even adorned donkey ears, much to the embarrassment of my children!).

This book is the result of a decade or so of my work in Church of England parish ministry. Many of these pieces have been written for church all-age services as well as "ordinary" Sundays, and school services. They were written to be read aloud and performed, so you may want to try this yourself!

Whether you're someone looking for fresh inspiration as you plan your own services, or a Christian looking for something to inspire your own worship and devotion, I hope this book is a blessing to you. May it fill you with living hope!

---

* Defined by Merriam-Webster as "a time when conditions are right for the accomplishment of a crucial action : the opportune and decisive moment". *Merriam-Webster Dictionary*, https://www.merriam-webster.com/dictionary/kairos

Living Hope is not designed to be read front-to-back like a novel. See it more as something to be dipped into and enjoyed.

Part 1 – Telling the Story

A collection of monologues and sketches that seek to tell the familiar story in a new way, often from the perspective of the characters involved. These would be perfect for use in services and would work as stand-alone pieces.

Part 2 – The Power of the Cross – Devotional Services for Good Friday

Reflections (written from the perspectives of the characters involved) and prayers and interspersed with Bible readings from the Passion narratives in the Gospels. These were written for "Last Hour" services, taking place at 2pm on Good Friday. The Bible readings are part of the text to help you in your own devotions.

Part 3 – Proclaiming Hope – The Message of Holy Week and Easter

Sermons I have preached over the years on Gospel passages on the Passion (the period between Palm Sunday and Good Friday) and Resurrection of Jesus. These have been preached on ordinary Sundays during Lent and Easter season as well as Good Friday and Easter Sunday. Some are interspersed with the monologues that you will find elsewhere in the book.

Part 4 - Easter for All Ages

These are some of the all age talks I've written for our services on Easter Sunday. Hopefully these will inspire and help those who have the wonderful but challenging task of leading services and are looking for something fresh to say.

Part 5 – Responding to Hope

Poetry, which often forms my personal expression of worship in this season. My greatest challenge as a "professional Christian" is that I can be so focused on communicating the Good News to others that I fail to appreciate its meaning for myself. These poems flow from those times when I stop, reflect and worship.

Part 6 – Journeying in Hope

A four-week devotional for Holy Week and Easter that starts on Palm Sunday, containing Bible verses I selected and reflections I wrote on Twitter. You may want to use this to accompany your own devotions, perhaps at the end of the day.

Please get in touch and let me know what you've found helpful, particularly if you've used any of these pieces in your own context. Get in touch via email – info@halwillpublishing.co.uk – I'd love to hear from you.

As I wrote, I genuinely believe I have one of the best jobs in the world. I love having the opportunity to express my creativity to tell other people about Jesus. I'm grateful to my church community, St Christopher's Allesley Park and Whoberley in Coventry, for your love and support over the years and putting up with some of my more whacky ideas; to the wonderful school community of St John's Church of England Academy, especially the brilliant children and also to the headteachers whom I've had the privilege of serving with – Andy Brown, Gary Watson and Laura Stevenson, who have been friends as well as colleagues. Thanks to Simon Ponsonby who saw my vocation as a writer, Sue Goodwin, who was a superb training minister and colleague, and the church communities of the St Philip's Werrington and St John's

Wetley Rocks, who gave me space to try things as I first stepped out in ordained ministry.

Thanks to all the preachers and authors, such as Adrian Plass, Tim Keller, Ian Paul, who have inspired my thinking, writing and creating on Holy Week and Easter. I want to mention Nick Page particularly, whose book *The Longest Week* completely revolutionised my understanding of this seminal week in world history and has inspired much of my own writing and thinking. I have tried to cite direct references, but I apologise if I've missed any out.

Thanks to my parents, who have been my editors-in-chief over the years; and to my mother-in-law, Janet Wilson, who has always been such an encouragement to me in my ministry. I want to especially thank my family – my wife, Liz, who gives me space and grace to do what I do and holds the family together while I'm busy with church things (Holy Week and Easter is not an easy time for vicarage families) and my children, who have been so supportive and among my biggest fans. I love you all.

Ultimately, my gratitude is to Jesus, my source of hope and salvation, my redeemer and rescuer. To him be the glory!

Andy March
Coventry
January 2023

PART 1
Telling the Story

A Donkey's Easter Tale

Hello, my name's Dave, the donkey. You won't know me … not many people do. You might know my Grandpa, Darrell. He's the one who went all the way from Nazareth – that's a long, long, long way away – and carried a young woman – who was very pregnant – all the way to Bethlehem. Her name was Mary, and she was carrying a very special baby, Jesus, who was God's baby. She had been chosen by God to be the mother of the new-born King and saviour of the world. My grandpa, Darrell, was so honoured to bear such a special burden.

Anyway, I'm here to tell you about something incredible that happened to me! I was in Bethany – that's near Jerusalem, in case you don't know – I was minding my own business eating grass, thinking very important donkey thoughts, and that sort of thing, when two complete strangers came up to me and untied me. My owners came out and asked them what these two were doing – I'm not surprised really, it's not every day that you get taken away – they could have been donkey-napping me! The two men said something very strange, "The Lord needs it." But that seemed be ok for my owners, who let them go. Someone important needed me – that was good enough. It's not every day *that* happens! But who was it? Who was so important, and why did he need me?

And then I met him. At first, he didn't look very important. He was dressed normally, but when I looked at him, he looked very kind, but a little sad too. There was something different about him. Something very special.

The men threw their coats on me, and then they put this man on my back. He rode me towards the great city of Jerusalem, and as we were walking along, people put coats on the road before us. There were lots of people – they all looked so excited and happy. They waved palm branches, shouted and cheered. They told each other stories of the wonderful things this man had done – he had healed the sick and done some amazing things. The people shouted out, "'Welcome! God bless the king who comes in the name of the Lord.' Peace in heaven and glory to God!"

I was amazed, the man on my back was a king? He was a king, coming into the city, and being welcomed by the people of the city. He didn't seem like a king, at least not the kind of king we were used to. He seemed so full of love, he seemed to really care for the people, and the people loved him. This king was called Jesus, and I carried him into Jerusalem. Me – Dave the donkey – it was the proudest moment of my life.

I said that the people loved him and welcomed him; well, some didn't love him – they looked very angry at what was happening and were whispering to each other. Not everyone was welcoming this king. In fact, I heard something awful. A few days later they had Jesus arrested and killed, even though he'd done nothing wrong. I couldn't believe it.

But then a rumour went round – he'd risen from the dead. That's amazing. My owners told me that he said this would happen, that it had to happen. It's been an amazing few days. I won't ever forget them, or the king I carried.

Summary to say afterwards …

Dave knew he carried someone special, he knew he carried a king, but he didn't know just how special Jesus was. When they put Jesus on the cross on Good Friday, it hurt. The people who did it were punishing Him for things that He never did, for Jesus never did anything wrong. Because God loved us and wanted to be friends with us, He took every one of our sins – you know, the things we do wrong – out of our hearts and put them into Jesus. Jesus felt all the sadness and loneliness that sin brings. Then Jesus died. But God brought Him back to life on Easter morning. And now we can be friends with God and enjoy life forever with him. That is why we celebrate Easter.

Miriam: The Widow at the Temple (based on Luke 20:27-21:4)

My husband Malachi died twenty years ago. So long ago now that I can barely recall his face. When he was alive, we were ok. We were never rich, but we got by – he was a stonemason by trade and the rebuilding of the temple, begun under old King Herod, meant that he was never out of work – many skilled hands were required to work on those incredible, gleaming, dressed white stones – and I may be biased, but there were few more skilled than Malachi. It was a great honour for him to be working on the house of the Lord – he was following in the footsteps of his hero Bezalel whose God-given talents had brought the Tabernacle into being in the days of Moses. In fact, Bezalel was the name of our son, who had no choice but to join his father's trade once he became of age – I swear that Malachi was counting down the days until that would happen; meanwhile he taught Bezalel all he knew, which was wonderful, although I wasn't totally convinced that an eight year old should be wielding a saw… how they didn't have any accidents I'll never know.

There were no accidents, until that day. They hadn't been working together on the temple – or their bit of it – for long – just a few months. Bezalel was not yet seventeen. I'll never forget their excitement as they got ready for work – they loved doing everything together – they were joking and laughing, Bezalel full of the confidence of youth, teasing his dad about the slowness of his work, Malachi replying that with such an important job as the work on the Lord's house, skill mattered more than speed. Bezalel always had to have the last word, so he countered in turn that he had both more skill and speed. They were still arguing about it when they left that morning, still bantering as they kissed me goodbye. And that was the last I saw of them. A man appeared in the middle of day, reported that there had been an accident. A timber hadn't been secured properly and the part of the wall they had been working on collapsed, crushing those working below. They were killed instantly.

At first the neighbours and my extended family helped out. But they moved on – they had their own lives and families to worry about. I was on my own, had to find my own way to survive. I was able to live in our family home, and sought to use what money Malachi had left me as wisely and well as possible, but I didn't know how long that would last or when the money would run out. I needed to rely on the Lord, my provider – he had a track record for looking after widows, which was just as well, as the temple authorities had no interest in looking after me whatsoever, even though it was on their premises, under their supervision, that my husband and my son were killed.

Despite all this, I go into the temple courts as often as I can. I feel closer to the Lord there, I feel his presence, even though as a woman, I'm not allowed very close to the holy of holies … but I also feel the presence of my husband and son. I go to the part of the temple that they'd worked on, lay my hands on the stone and feel the marks of the chisels, imagine their strength and skill at work. When I'm in the temple courts I don't feel alone – they're always crowded with pilgrims from all over the world, and traders selling their wares, especially at festival time. This Passover time was no different, with what must have been thousands of people thronging the area around the temple. I wove my way from my home in the lower city, through the narrow sheets, politely shaking my head at the people who were trying to sell me all sorts of things, to the public pools, so I could make sure I was ritually clean, through the Triple Gate up the underground passageway leading to the temple court itself and then out onto the dazzling brightness and the noise of the Court of the Gentiles, all of your senses are accosted at once, with the light – the white and gold of the temple building radiating the light of the sun, and the sound – the mingling of voices from the cries of market stall sellers to the normal buzz of conversation, and in the background the noises of the animals which were waiting to be sacrificed. Being confronted with all this all at once was a bewildering experience. I took a moment, took a deep breath and made my way through the crowd in the courts of the Gentiles to the court of women, where I would make my offering, which was my main reason for being there that day. As I walked towards the main entrance of the temple itself, I noticed a crowd clustered together in one place, which wasn't unusual in itself, but what was unusual was the fact that they were quiet. At first I dismissed it – you often get Rabbis who seek to draw a crowd, the teachers of the law love to get attention in their flowing robes and impressive prayers; I recognised the voice of one of them as he was speaking – he was a Sadducee – they're the ones in charge of the temple business, because that's what it is. They have their disagreements with the Pharisees over whether there's life after death. They only believe in the Torah, and as there's no hint of this there, they argue that this life, this world, is all there is. It's alright for them to believe this – their life is comfortable, isn't it? They're rich. They have the best of the world. I stopped and listened, intrigued to hear what he was going to say – he seemed to be in debate with a man I didn't recognise. "Teacher," he said, "'Moses wrote for us that if a man's brother dies and leaves a wife but no children, the man must marry the widow and raise up offspring for his brother. Now there were seven brothers. The first one married a woman and died childless. The second and then the third married her, and in the same way the seven died, leaving no children. Finally, the woman died too. Now then, at the resurrection whose wife will she be, since the seven were married to her?"

It didn't take a genius to work out that this was a trick question, a riddle, an attempt to make the teacher look stupid.

The fact they used the plight of a woman, a widow, who was passed from one man to another, as the subject of their theological riddle was also a sign of how little they cared about the everyday problems of people like me, who do our best to survive. I wonder whether he knows that people like us really exist. But if he did, it wouldn't matter, because we have no power. What about this mysterious teacher, how would he answer? I watched him as he listened to them – at first he seemed to take them absolutely seriously, but then he seemed to roll his eyes and he began looking around at the crowd – and, somehow, his gaze met mine and, I couldn't believe it, but I'm pretty sure that he winked and smiled at me. It was a look of sympathy and understanding that seemed to say that despite what the Sadducees implied, I did matter, that I wasn't just the object of some riddle, that God saw and cared about my plight. In that moment I felt like I had worth and dignity. It's a long time since I'd last felt that.

He waited until the man finished, paused, as if he were giving his question serious consideration and proceeded to destroy the argument completely.

He quoted the Torah – the Sadducees' own base text – and implied that by The Lord saying, 'I am the God of Abraham, Isaac and Jacob', all these were somehow still alive at the time of Moses. In other words, he accused these men – the fundamentalist scripture party – of not having read their scriptures. To be honest these theological debates do go over my head rather, but I sensed he was simply saying, "God has the power to sort all this out. What makes you think the resurrected life is going to be like things down here?" You see, when he talked about the resurrection, about new life, you could tell there was no doubt that he believed in the world to come. When he talked, it gave me real hope. Though we will die, we will rise, and that new life will be wonderful. Though my dear Malachi and Bezalel are dead – and how I miss them, they will rise. I will see them again. We are children of the resurrection, because our God is the God of the covenant – of the promises he made to Abraham, Isaac, Jacob, and Moses too – he is the God of the living, so not even death can break this covenant. I don't claim to understand it, but I do believe it, that there is hope.

Well, the crowd loved this – the Sadducees beaten at their own game – I even heard some of the other teachers of the law cry out, "Well said, teacher!" and the Sadducees fell silent. I enjoyed that! But this teacher wasn't done yet. He began to speak about the Messiah, our promised rescuer, who will come one day to deliver our nation and restore the kingdom. He asked how such a figure could be a "son" or descendant of David if he would become David's Lord. Maybe he was questioning whether we have the right understanding of what the Messiah is and what he would do? Maybe he isn't going to battle the Romans or restore David's Kingdom? Later, I heard that this teacher had spoken lots about a different Kingdom – the Kingdom of God. I wonder if he means the Messiah would bring in this Kingdom instead- a Kingdom where people are all shown as precious to God, stand equal in his eyes, where power and status are shown for the false gods that they are.

I dragged myself away at that point and headed towards the court of the women, where I could make my offering. As I left I heard the teacher make some scathing remark about the teachers of the law and their flowing robes. Power and status obviously mean far less to him than they do to them. They love to be recognised, lauded, rewarded, and have been known to exploit people, relying on the hospitality of those who have barely enough to live on. I know; I've been there.

I'd brought two copper coins with me for my offering, which I gave at the same time as some significantly richer people – you could tell they were wealthy by the clothes they wore – and they seemed to be very keen on people seeing just how generous they were. I felt embarrassed to be putting in just those two coins, but it was really all I had to give – actually, it's all I have to live on. Why should I hold back? I believe that my God has been incredibly generous to me. He's not held back from me, so I shouldn't hold back from him. He deserves all my love and all my devotion. I turned and made my way out of the court of women, and on my way out saw the teacher again. He was with a smaller group of people now. He looked at me and smiled, and spoke to what I assume were his disciples. 'Truly I tell you,' he said, 'this poor widow has put in more than all the others. All these people gave their gifts out of their wealth; but she out of her poverty put in all she had to live on.'

We exchanged glances again as I walked past, towards the Court of the Gentiles. I know I was blushing to have been singled out for such incredible praise. How did he know my life's situation? How could he see how difficult it's been all these years? Somehow, he knew. He saw into my heart. I love my Lord. My God is all I live for. Though others don't see that – all they see is my garb, my poverty, but my God sees and knows, and somehow, this man does too. What's inside my beating, burning heart is what matters to God. This man seemed to see all that, and saw fit to give me honour and dignity, to say that God is pleased with me and my devotion when I offer myself fully and freely to him. I have nothing to offer God but myself, and I think he accepts this with all his heart.

Something beautiful for Jesus (based on Mark 14:1-11)

I've been asked many times about that week. A week like no other. I've been asked about the excitement at being swept up among those joyful crowds as Jesus entered Jerusalem, acclaimed as King. And yes, it felt pretty amazing to have been at the centre of the joy that day – we felt like we could take on the world. I've also been asked about *that* Friday, although, honestly, I don't have much to say. To my shame I was in Bethany with the others, in hiding, awaiting news. When the news came – it still hurts now – to hear how he'd died and how we'd run away in Gethsemane – yes, we were terrified – and with good reason – but we shouldn't have left him alone. Of course, what happened on that Sunday unexpectedly, wonderfully, changed everything – but more on that another time.

What stands out to me about that week wasn't so much what Jesus said or did in public, but the private moments away from the crowds, particularly the meals. You see, Jesus loved eating – and he didn't seem to mind who he ate with. He just loved to share food with people – in fact, he got a bit of a reputation with certain religious leaders who thought he should have been more discerning about the company he kept around the dinner table. He ate with *sinners*, they sneered. They were scandalised by the idea that God might be interested in the so-called dregs of society who were, in their eyes, beyond saving, but Jesus saw these people as broken, hurting – and certainly within the reach of God's transforming love. No one is beyond God's love. No one is beyond redemption – Jesus showed us that – gave us regular lessons in this as day after day, the broken and hurting, forgotten and abandoned, found love, dignity and hope when they met him. They've become part of the family, part of the ragtag community that Jesus formed.

We were based in Bethany that week, a short walk from Jerusalem. Martha, Mary and Lazarus were the generous hosts – nothing was too much for them when it came to Jesus, not after he'd raised Lazarus back to life. Jesus saw their home as a sanctuary, a place where he could relax, centre himself and recover from the often bruising encounters he had in the temple precincts, sparring with the religious leaders. He'd told us about these debates before, when he'd visited Jerusalem before, but it was something else witnessing them first-hand that week – it was clear they weren't interested in debate; no, they had more sinister motives – they were out to trip him up, discredit it him – it seemed nasty at the time – of course, we had no idea just what they were prepared to do to bring him down. Each day that week, it got more intense, more difficult, and you could tell it was taking it out of Jesus. So, he was grateful for the sanctuary and safety that Bethany offered – and that he could be himself with those who loved him, who'd journeyed with him these past few years.

That night, Wednesday, it was, we were actually in Simon's house for a meal. I don't remember the details of the conversation – we were probably just reflecting on the latest debates we'd heard – we'd just finished our meal, and were probably in that post-meal sleepy state when suddenly Mary came in with an alabaster jar of perfume. Before we knew it, she broke the jar and poured it over Jesus's head as he was reclining at the table – I think he was taken by surprise as much as we were. The smell was overwhelming, filling our senses. At first there was a pause – we were all a little bit in shock – but then Judas Iscariot almost shouted,

There was no need for that! Why did she waste all that perfume? It could have been sold for more than a year's wages[a] and the money given to the poor.'

And then he turned to Mary – "That's so typical of you, Mary – you're always so over the top – and you've gone too far now."

But then, Jesus, his gaze fixed on Mary, who was almost cowering in the corner, spoke quietly but with absolute authority. 'Leave her alone. Why are you bothering her? She has done such a beautiful thing to me. You will have the poor with you every day for the rest of your lives. You can feel free to help them any time you want. But you will not always have me. She did what she could when she could. She poured perfume on my body beforehand to prepare for my burial. You can be sure that wherever the Message is preached throughout the world, what she has done will also be told, in memory of her.'

No one really knew what to say then. I can't say we fully understood what had happened – we didn't realise the significance of what Mary did that night or why it touched Jesus's heart – not until afterwards, that is. You see, women are second-class citizens. You're grateful to be born a man or to have sons – that's the kind of society we live in – but Jesus disregarded all that – he had given Mary – and others too – dignity, respect, purpose and acceptance – and I think that part of her act was an expression of gratitude. She wanted to say thank you in the way that only Mary could.

But there was more to the anointing than just a sense of gratitude – and Jesus connected with this – there was grief in Mary's face. She could see what we couldn't, even though Jesus had told us enough times by then – she could see that Jesus was going to be punished – she realised that those in power in that temple were out to get Jesus – they wouldn't allow him to get away with challenging the status quo in the way that he had. No, they would punish him and make him pay the ultimate price. Mary saw it in a way that none of us could – perhaps it was because she herself as a woman, knew what it was to be downtrodden – she knew the cost of trying to break free. And she knew that this would end in his death, expressing her love and compassion for him in a way that only she could. Jesus was right – it was a beautiful act, and deserves to be remembered. Whenever I get the whiff of perfume, I'm taken back to that extraordinary night. I remember her worship, I remember how much it delighted Jesus, and I wonder what beautiful thing I can do for Jesus, because I want to delight him too.

A Thief in Paradise (inspired by Luke 23:39-43)

Wow, where am I? It's so beautiful here, it's so beautiful here.

What am I doing here? Where am I?

Oh, hello, I didn't see you there. I can't take it in … My name is Levi, and I'm not a good man. No, I'm really not. I've done some horrible things. I've stolen, hurt people, I even killed someone. I never intended that, it kind of happened.

Anyway, I got caught. The Romans nabbed me, beat me. We all know what happens to criminals who get caught by the Romans. Those crosses, those awful crosses – everywhere. Soon I'd be on one, and to be honest, I deserved it – deserved everything that came to me.

Three of us were up on those crosses being crucified that day. One was like me – a robber – a bandit, getting his just desserts, just like me. The other one was different – a political prisoner. Claimed to be a King – and we all know the only *true* king around here was the emperor. Anyway, rumour has it that this guy, Jesus, had been very badly treated, that he hadn't done anything wrong – just stitched up by the Jewish leaders.

Crucifixion is awful. The worst possible punishment. The beatings are bad enough, but then they nail you to that cross. While we were being nailed, me and this other robber bloke were swearing and cursing, wishing we'd never been born. Jesus at first, didn't say a word, but then he did. It was amazing. "Father, forgive them," he said, "They don't know what they're doing." That's incredible. How can he say that? He was innocent; it was a disgrace the way they'd treated him. Yet, he could ask God to forgive them? They didn't deserve it, they deserved to be punished, just like us. And yet he forgave them, just like he's forgiven me. That's incredible.

Anyway, this man had to put up with dead awful insults being thrown at him. Dreadful what they said. They mocked him and spat at him. Again he said nothing, took it all on the chin. Didn't get bitter or angry. And then the other guy started joining in. He was so bitter and angry. He sneered at Jesus, "if you're who you say you are, why don't you save us and yourself. As if you could." And he laughed, a hollow, bitter laugh.

I'd kept my mouth shut until then, but I couldn't stand it anymore – how could they do this to this bloke. He'd done nothing wrong! I turned to the other thief and said, "don't you fear God? You should do! You and I are guilty as sin. We've paid the price, we deserve to be here. But this man has done nothing wrong! He's innocent. Just leave him alone."

I don't know why I said the next bit, but something in him gave me hope – hope for someone like me. So, I turned to Jesus and said, "Jesus, remember me when you come into your kingdom." I knew he was a King, but not the usual sort of King. And I knew he was the only hope that I could possibly have. I wasn't expecting much; I didn't deserve much good to happen to me – I was expecting him to reject me like everyone else had.

But he said something incredible; something I will never forget and always be thankful for. He turned to me and said, "today you'll be with me in paradise."

Me, a crook, a murderer, a scumbag, an awful, awful man, in paradise. I don't deserve it. I don't deserve to be loved in such a way. And yet, here I am. A thief in paradise. – and it's amazing. Why am I here? Because a crucified King opened the door and let me in. There is hope for people even like me – and it's amazing!

The Centurion

My name is Marcus Justus Loginus. I am a centurion of the Sebastii cohort based at Herod's fortress in Jerusalem. It's our job to keep the peace. Not an easy task when it's Jewish festival season. Hundreds of thousands of people flock from all over the country for their celebrations – and there's almost always trouble. They get together and sing their songs of freedom. Let them sing – there's no hope of them getting freedom any time soon, not while we Romans are here – but it doesn't stop them trying! We know it's coming now – we're used to snuffing out any rebellion before it has any chance of getting going. The ringleaders are arrested, whipped and then crucified. This generally nips the trouble in the bud.

Crucifixion is horrible – the guy who came up with the idea must have been really warped. It's so horrible we can't use it for Roman citizens. No, it's the slaves' death – reserved for them and foreign rebels. Sends out a message to everyone that they need to behave. Anyway, we dealt with three of them that day. Two of them were pretty standard – they were bandits and murderers. Caught red-handed. They were shouting and cursing and screaming blue murder as we crucified them. But there was something different about the third man. We were expecting another man, Barabbas, who was another murderer, but then this bloke Jesus appeared. He'd been arrested in the middle of the night, hastily tried and sentenced to death because he claimed to be king. We all know there's no king apart from Caesar! I don't think Pilate, our governor thought that Jesus was any trouble really and he tried to have him freed, but   the local rulers weren't having it. They wanted rid of Jesus no matter what and they promised him trouble if he didn't give in. So, Pilate agreed. The rulers stitched him up, if you ask me. He was an innocent man.

Well, of course, as soon they heard Jesus had claimed to be king – and, rumour has it that he says he's the Son of God, the lads in my troop had a field day – twisted together a crown of thorns and forced it on his head, dressed him up in a robe and then bowed down, saying, "hail, King of the Jews!" – this was on top of the normal insults they threw at their prisoners. They then whipped him extra brutally – we're from Samaria, you see. Samaritans *hate* Jews, especially those who think they're kings. I suppose you could say the way we treated him was sick, but we knew no different. Normally our victims shout and scream and curse, but he never said a word, you know. Nothing. He was silent. Wouldn't rise to our abuse.

So, after mocking and beating him, we led him out to Skull Hill, just outside the city. He was too weak to carry the cross himself, so we got someone from the crowd to carry it for him. And we crucified him – with those two bandits. When he was up there, people hurled insults on him. The other people we were crucifying joined in too.

All the while he said very little. And the words he did say will be words I'll never forget. As we were nailing him to the cross, he managed to say, "Father, forgive them. They don't what they're doing." Wow. I didn't think much of it then, but the more I think of it, the more it amazes me. Here was a man who was innocent, who'd been brutally treated and mocked, and crucified, uttering words of forgiveness to the very people who'd put him there.

At about noon, something really strange happened – the sky went pitch black. It was spooky. That sort of thing is a sign of doom. Somehow, I knew that this darkness was to do with Jesus. Something was going on that was bigger than the death of a common criminal. It stayed dark for about 3 hours, and then Jesus gave a loud cry and died.

I'd watched him all that day. He'd gone through such horror, it was unimaginable, and yet never once did he rise to bitterness or anger. Amazing! I've watched many men die, and I can tell you there was something different about him. He was no ordinary criminal, no ordinary man. I knew he was special, so I cried out, "Surely, he was the Son of God."

"Father, forgive them," he said. "Father, forgive them." God knows the terrible things I've done, the blood on my hands. I don't deserve to be forgiven, and yet that man, Jesus, forgave all those who killed him. That includes me. Could it be that I've been forgiven too? That all the terrible things I've done in my life have been wiped away? Could it be that I can have a brand-new start, that these bloodied hands might be able to be clean once more?

Jairus' Daughter

Part 1

My name is Tamar, the daughter of Jairus and Abigail, and I'm nearly eight years old. I'm no one very special, but something very special happened to me. It didn't start very well. I got very poorly. I felt hot and sweaty, then cold and sweaty, I didn't want to eat or get out of bed – or do anything really. At first my mummy and daddy weren't worried – they thought it was just a passing fever. But I didn't get better – in fact, I got worse. I was even too poorly to be bored. After a week, my parents started to get really worried. The doctor came round, but just shook his head. Mum and Dad tried to hide it, but I could tell from their faces that they were scared. I asked them if I was going to get better, and they told me I would, but I didn't believe them – and I knew they didn't either. They did that really annoying thing that grown-ups do – talking about me when they were in the same room as if I wasn't there – I didn't really understand what they were saying. All I heard was them mentioning something about going to fetch a man called Jesus – he was the only one who could help. So, daddy left in a hurry. I'd never seen him like that.

I don't remember much after that. I must have fallen asleep. I had these amazing dreams filled with such love and joy – they were amazing. The next thing I heard was this voice. "Little girl, get up!" It said. I opencd my eyes, shook my head, and got up. I felt like I'd been woken out of the deepest of sleeps. This kind looking man was sitting by my bed, holding my hand – and there were two men with him that I didn't know, but also mummy and daddy. They looked so happy – they had tears in their eyes. I was confused at first, but then they told me what had happened – I'd actually died, but the kind man, Jesus had brought me back from the dead. I was a miracle.

He didn't stay long, but long enough for my mummy and daddy to say thank you to him about a million times! He just smiled and told them to get me something to eat.

From that day our whole family became his followers – we spent as much time as we could with him and saw the amazing things he did, and heard the amazing things he said. It was amazing – and very exciting. We knew there was something special about him – after all, no one else could do the things he did. Who was he?

Part 2

One day, a year later, we all went to Jerusalem together. It was very exciting. Mummy and Daddy talked about him coming into Jerusalem to become King, that he would rule now and we'd no longer have to be afraid of the horrid Romans. That sounded wonderful. Those Roman soldiers were so scary, with their helmets and swords – not like Jesus, who was so kind and loving. When Jesus came into the city, he was riding a donkey and there were loads of people in the crowd to welcome him, singing out songs of praise – Praise the Lord – here comes the King! We were all waving palm branches. It was so exciting!

But then, later that week, we heard that there were people who didn't like Jesus, who didn't want him to be king. In fact, they wanted to do horrible things to him. They wanted to kill him. That's impossible, I thought, after all, I know he's not scared of death – I'm alive because of him! Again, my parents started to get really worried. They tried to hide it, but I knew. Then came that Thursday – a day I will never forget. We had a meal all together, then Jesus said some strange things about the bread and wine we were eating being his body and blood given for us. I didn't understand what he meant at all. I just noticed that everyone else suddenly became very sad. It made me sad too. At the end of the meal we went to the place we were staying and I want to bed. Later that night, I was woken up by mummy and daddy talking. I pretended to be asleep, but I heard them saying that Jesus had been arrested. Powerful people wanted to kill him and there wasn't anything anyone could do to stop them. It didn't seem possible at all. I didn't sleep well that night.

The next morning – it was Friday – mummy and daddy were crying. Jesus had been killed. We were all so sad. It was so unfair – he'd never done anything wrong. Poor Jesus. They had hurt him badly. Been horrible to him. How could they? We were also sad, because everyone had been so happy when he was around. But all that had gone.

The next day we all cried and cried. I was so cross that people could be so horrid.

Part 3

On Sunday, we heard some amazing news – when mummy's friends Mary went to see where Jesus had been buried, his body had gone. They didn't know where. But then, Mary saw Jesus. He was alive! It was amazing. I didn't believe her – I thought it was a story made to make us feel better, but then later on, we were all together and – there he was – he appeared in the room – he was alive. I was so excited and ran to him, to give him a hug! He was alive. He made us all so happy! Because of Jesus we can all be happy. We don't need to feel sad any more.

Mary Magdalene – The day everything changed (based on John 20:1-18)

I made my way numbly to the tomb that Sunday morning. I hadn't slept a wink since Friday, when my world fell apart, when I saw my Lord being laid to rest in that cold, dark tomb. I spent most of the time since then weeping. That man, my Rabbi, wasn't just any other man; he was the one on whom I had pinned my hopes. And I watched him die. It was so awful.

Before he came along, I was nothing – an outcast, plagued by seven demons; evil spirits that raged inside me – voices I neither recognised nor wanted to recognise. They wouldn't leave me alone. And then Jesus released me; he allowed me to hope again. So I followed him and witnessed incredible things. As well as that amazing teaching he performed incredible miracles: he healed the sick, cast out demons and even raised the dead. Amazing. Surely this man was the Messiah – the promised king who would rescue the Jewish people from all of their oppressors. As time passed, my hopes grew – my hopes and all of the others too. Only last week he entered Jerusalem riding on a donkey as the crowds shouted, "Hosanna to the Son of David! Blessed is he who comes in the name of the Lord!"

The excitement grew … and then … and then … I could scarcely believe it … it all went horribly wrong. The reports came on Friday morning that he had been arrested and the next thing I knew I was watching him die. Crucifixion was an awful thing, but it was even worse when the man being crucified was the man you'd loved and on whom you'd pinned all your hopes. People mocked him, saying that he should save himself if he were the Son of God – and I hoped that he'd do just that – after all, I knew he had the power to. And I continued hoping, but that hope got smaller and smaller the shallower his breathing got. And then finally, he breathed his last with a final cry, "It is finished" and my hope had gone. I was devastated. It was all over.

The rest of that day are a blur really. Me and the other Marys, and Salome, who'd been with him when he was dying, we began to wonder what would happen to Jesus now. Who would look after him? Thankfully a kind man, Joseph of Arimathea said he would ensure Jesus was laid in his own family tomb. He arranged for Jesus' body to be taken down from the cross, and took it to the grave. We followed; we wanted to know where they would lay him, so we could pay our last respects and care for him. We went back to our lodgings in the city and got spices and ointment ready to anoint his body. But the Sabbath was just starting, so we had to rest. It was so hard. We were reeling from all that had happened, all that we had lost.

Early on the Sunday morning, we went to the tomb. This was our chance to serve Jesus one last time, by giving the body the care it deserved. But the stone had been moved – Jesus body was no longer there! As if Jesus hadn't undergone enough already, now his body had been stolen. It added insult to awful injury. I ran to tell Simon Peter and the disciple Jesus loved, saying, "They have taken the Lord out of the tomb, and we don't know where they have put him!"

Impulsive Peter and the other disciple didn't believe me, of course, and ran off to check out my story. I was left behind. In bits. Now I was weeping, not simply because Jesus was dead, but because they'd stolen his body. The one thing that had been left to me – the simple act of giving his body the treatment he deserved – even that had been taken away from me. My head was spinning. I didn't know what else to do, so I went back to the tomb, stumbling there through the tears. Why? Because I probably didn't have anywhere else to go. I felt that by being at the tomb, I would somehow feel closer to Jesus.

But then, something very unexpected happened. I was standing outside the tomb, weeping. I bent over to look into the tomb, double checking I wasn't imagining it all, and there were two angels in white there, seated where Jesus' body had been, one at the head and the other at the foot. They asked me why I was crying, so I told them, "They have taken my Lord away and I don't know where they have put him."

I don't think I was really comprehending I was talking with angels – not your everyday occurrence, is it? All I could think about was the fact my Lord's body had gone. It was all too much – shock, grief, bewilderment – were all swirling round my mind.

Suddenly I saw someone in the corner of my eye – perhaps he could help. I didn't know who he was, I couldn't see properly, my eyes were so blurred by tears.

He asked me, "Woman, why are you crying? Who is it you are looking for?"

I thought he was the gardener; I wasn't sure who else would be hanging around. Perhaps he had something to do with the disappearance of Jesus' body? "Sir, if you have carried him away, tell me where you have put him, and I will get him."

Everything changed with one word. "Mary." The penny finally dropped. It dawned on me who this man was – that the man who'd set me free from those demons, who'd taught incredible things and done wonderful works and who I'd watched die just two days previously; this was the man who wonderfully, incredibly, but truly, was alive. I couldn't believe it. All I wanted to do was hold on to him and never let go, to stay in this moment, hoping it would never end.

Jesus extracted himself from me with a smile. "Mary, don't cling on to me. I need you to go and tell my disciples. Tell them that I've risen from the grave, just as I said I would. So, I tore myself away from Jesus, then rushed off back to Jesus' disciples, with this most incredible news, "I have seen the Lord!"

Peter's Story

This has been inspired by the Gospel accounts of the Resurrection and also the following verses:

For what I received I passed on to you as of first importance: that Christ died for our sins according to the Scriptures, that he was buried, that he was raised on the third day according to the Scriptures, and that **he appeared to Peter**, *and then to the Twelve.*
(1 Corinthians 15:3-5, emphasis mine.)

Let's listen together to Peter's story.

- - - -

I didn't sleep a wink. I couldn't. I felt so awful. Sick in the pit of my stomach. Those words he had said to me kept going round my head. "Tonight, before the cock crows, you'll deny you've ever known me." I couldn't believe it! Me, Peter, the one he'd nicknamed Rocky, deny Jesus? I'd never deny Jesus. Never. As if I could. He was the man who had given me purpose. Life was so exciting when he was around. I'd made lots of mistakes, but he forgave every one – amazing really. How could I ever deny the man who'd turned my life upside down? Who'd allowed me to share in the greatest adventure ever? I couldn't!

But I did. Three times. Swore I didn't have the faintest idea who he was. And then he looked at me. He wasn't angry; he was reproachful. Disappointed. If I'm honest, that's worse. I was devastated. I couldn't believe I'd let Jesus down. I'd been so full of it. So full of good words and good intentions. But I couldn't back them up with my actions. I was so ashamed of myself, I ran out and wept. Wept like I've never wept before.

Friday was even worse. When Jesus needed his friends most, we deserted him – all of us, except John and some of the women in our group. It was fear that kept me away. What if they got me too and treated me the way they treated him? The one place I wanted to be was by Jesus' side – showing him that he could still depend on me and my support, yet I was too much of a coward.

So, I had to rely on others to keep me posted. And the news got worse and worse as the day wore on. First, they told me that he'd been put on trial for blasphemy, that the authorities wanted his blood; then, I heard about the beating, the insults, the scourging; and then they told me he'd been sentenced to death. Crucifixion. A death so horrible that Roman citizens are spared such awful treatment. Finally, I heard the news I thought I would never hear – he'd died.

Jesus. The miracle maker. My hero. My captain. My leader. The one who was going to save us all from oppression. Dead.

I was numb. Devastated. Didn't believe it. My hopes were snuffed out with him. What was I going to do now? Where would I go?

Did you hear that I actually cut a man's ear off on Thursday night? One of the party who came to arrest Jesus. The man had it coming, if you asked me, but still, it wasn't a very clever thing to do. But Jesus healed him there and then. That's the kind of guy he was. That's why I couldn't believe that he'd died. You see, a man who could heal people in the blink of an eye. A man who could stop a storm. A man who could raise the dead. Well, that sort of man could save himself couldn't he? He couldn't be dead? So, why did he let them do that to him? Why did he let them kill him?

Saturday dragged on. I was exhausted, but couldn't sleep; hungry, but couldn't stomach anything. A small number of Jesus' followers gathered together in secret. We cried on each other's shoulders, basically. I found out from Mary Magdalene where he'd been buried. A man called Joseph of Arimathea gave up his tomb for Jesus' body to rest. I wanted to go there, to be with Jesus one last time, but it was the Sabbath, so we couldn't go anywhere. I would have to wait until today to pay my last respects to Jesus.

But then, this morning, something extraordinary happened. Mary Magdalene came and told me that the stone blocking the entrance had been rolled away. The tomb was empty. What? Empty? How was that possible? She told me to go and see for myself. So that's what I did.

I ran to the tomb with John to check it out. To make sure that the extreme emotion we'd all experienced hadn't got to Mary's head too much. I could not believe it. She was right – the tomb was empty. I went straight into the tomb and there were the grave clothes. But no body. It had gone. Where was Jesus? Why was the tomb empty? Who moved the stone?

Could the impossible have happened? Could Jesus be alive? I could scarcely believe it. It was simply too good to be true. After all, dead men don't rise from the dead. Do they?

Later, things got even more incredible! Mary told me that she'd met with Jesus face to face – that she'd mistaken him for the gardener at first, but then she knew it was him once he'd called her by name. Perhaps it was true after all. Maybe Jesus was alive! Maybe he had defeated death!

You're not going to believe the next thing that happened! I met with him face to face! He appeared right in front of me. Out of nowhere. It was really him. I could see the scars and everything. At first, all the feelings of shame and guilt came flooding back. I couldn't look him straight in the eye – how could I – I'd let him down so badly. But then he spoke to me. He reassured me that he forgave me. That I could start over again. He told me that I was still Rocky, that I still had a part to play in the great adventure he's planned for me. In fact, he told me that there were even more incredible days ahead. He said that the adventure was only just beginning and that he would walk with me and show me the way!

Suddenly I feel more excited than ever. I can't believe that so much has happened in so little time. I can't wait to tell the other disciples that I've seen Jesus and that he's alive! Back from the dead. God is truly at work in amazing ways. Jesus is alive! He has risen! I feel more alive than ever. If the adventure's only just begun, then bring it on!

Emmaus: The Road to Hope

I'd not slept a wink for two nights, not since our hopes were ripped to shreds by the Temple authorities and the Roman killing machine. I was still in shock in all honesty – all had happened so quickly. Could it be less than a week since Jesus had come in triumph to Jerusalem, acclaimed as the King he so clearly was? How was it possible that he was dead, just five days later? I was mulling over this when I heard a commotion from downstairs. Bleary eyed, I pulled on my clothes and went out to find out what was going on.

The two women, Mary Magdalene and Mary, my wife, were there and the disciples were huddled around them. Everyone looked flustered. Peter was

"It's empty, you're absolutely sure about this?" – that was Peter.

"Yes, we're sure."

"Empty?"

"Yes!"

"And you are absolutely sure you went to the right place."

"Yes!" replied, Mary Magdalene – you could tell she was exasperated. "We watched as they took down Jesus's body from the cross, and we followed those two Jerusalem disciples, Joseph of Arimathea and Nicodemus … all the way to the tomb. We saw them lay him there. We saw them seal the tomb with that great stone. We saw everything. The tomb is empty, we're telling you!"

Peter and the others stood, hands on hips, shaking their heads. "But where's his body then?"

Mary Magdalene replied, "We already told you, the angels told us he's alive. He is risen!" You could tell she was upset.

"Well, I don't believe it." Thomas exclaimed, "It's nonsense. Dead men don't rise from the dead."

Then Peter spoke up, "I'm going to go to see for myself – anyone else coming with me?"

John replied, "I'll go, although there shouldn't be too many of us, it's not safe."

"I'm coming with you," said Mary Magdalene.

And so they left. Peter and John came back about half an hour later and said that the women's story was true – the tomb was empty. But there was no sign of Jesus anywhere. Where was his body?

We simply didn't know what to do. One thing I was sure of, I couldn't just stay all day waiting. Life had to move on. I needed to get out, to clear my head. I found my wife, Mary, "I'm going to head home for a bit, check everything's ok. I won't stay long."

"Ok, darling, take Simeon with you. You could probably do with the company."

So, Simeon and I trudged off together. We relaxed as soon as we left the confines of the city, less worried about people following us. We filled the time talking about everything that had happened that whirlwind week. We were so engrossed that it was a while before we noticed we had company on the road, as a man drew up beside us. We couldn't see his face, because he was wearing a hood, for protection from the dust and dirt.

"What are you talking about together as you walk along?" he asked?

We stopped and our heads hung low. "Don't you know what's been happening in Jerusalem in the past few days? You're probably the only visitor who hasn't heard about it.

"Heard about what?" the stranger asked, apparently nonplussed.

"About Jesus of Nazareth," I answered. "He was a prophet who said and did many powerful things before God and all the people. The chief priests and our rulers handed him over to be sentenced to death, and they crucified him. The thing is, we had hoped that he was the one who was going to redeem Israel. It's now three days since all this took place.

Then, to cap it all, some of the women in our group amazed us. They went to the tomb early this morning but didn't find his body. They came and told us that they had seen a vision of angels, who said he was alive. Then some of our companions went to the tomb and found it just as the women had said, but they did not see Jesus."

To say we weren't expecting the next bit was an understatement. "You're so foolish! So slow! Why can't you believe everything the prophets spoke about?" The Messiah had to suffer these things and then enter his glory – it had to be this way." And the stranger started at the beginning, with the Books of Moses, and went on through all the Prophets, pointing out everything in the Scriptures that referred to the Messiah.

Before we knew it, we had nearly arrived at the village. "We're nearly home," I said,

"Oh," said the man, "I'm continuing on."

"Please don't", I replied, "Come in and stay with us. It's nearly evening – the day's almost over. Please stay."

The man agreed.

We went in and I hastily prepared some food for us and our guest. I was in a daze. What an extraordinary walk that had been.

We sat down together, and the man took the bread, gave thanks, broke it and began to give it to us.

And suddenly, in a flood of joy and amazement, it all became clear. It was Jesus! He'd been walking with us all along! How hadn't we seen it?

Then, Jesus disappeared. Vanished before our eyes.

We sat, looking at each other for a moment, speechless.

"That was – " Simeon started,

"Jesus, I know," I finished for him. "When he was talking with us on the road and opening the Scriptures to us, it was incredible, my heart felt like it was on fire!"

"Well, what are we waiting for?" Simeon exclaimed, "We have to go back to Jerusalem to tell the others."

And so we got up straightaway and almost ran back to where the disciples were all gathered. We'd met with the risen Jesus; impossibly wonderfully, he was alive. If we hadn't witnessed him breaking the bread, we wouldn't have believed it. I wondered what the others would say, and if they'd believe us, but I needn't have worried. There was an utter transformation in the room.

"It's true!" John almost shouted, "The Lord has risen and has appeared to Simon."

We exchanged our stories of transformation. The Lord has risen, and he's changed everything. What a difference a day makes!

Peter and the Miraculous Catch of Fish (based on John 21:1-14)

153

There are some numbers that stick in your head. My wife wishes there were other numbers that would do that for me - like birthdays; anniversary, that sort of thing, but they don't seem to. I could never retain that sort of information but with him it was different. I could remember all the numbers - the 12 he called - and the 11 that were left, 5,000 men and a whole bunch of women and children that he fed with just 5 loaves and 2 fish; and the 12 basketfuls of loaves left over – now that was incredible – and 153. That was the number of fish we caught the day he changed everything – again.

Jesus did that, you see, changed lives completely, turned them upside down. That's what he did for me, ever since I met him out fishing and he called me to drop everything and follow him to fish for people – and I did, and never regretted it – after all, he was the Messiah, the anointed Rescuer of Israel – the one who had the words of eternal life and his words and actions were full of such power, until he was arrested and everything fell apart. I struck out that night, took off a man's ear. I couldn't leave Jesus behind though, not completely, so I followed the soldiers at a safe distance all the way into the place where they were holding him while he awaited trial. Despite my best efforts I was recognised. I think my accent gave me away. They asked me if I knew Jesus. To my shame I denied ever having known him. Three times. That's another number I remember, much as I try to forget that one. I fled then and disappeared into the shadows, leaving Jesus to face whatever laid ahead of him alone. I didn't sleep that night and was in agony the next day, that Friday when I learned he had been sentenced to be crucified and then, finally, awfully, that he was dead. It was over.

But then, two days later the women came back from the tomb saying that Jesus was alive. We didn't believe them – of course we didn't – dead people don't rise from the dead. But I went to the tomb to check out their story and indeed, the tomb was empty just as they said, but there was no sign of Jesus. And then Jesus did appear – to me. I met with him face to face! He appeared right in front of me. Out of nowhere. It was really him. I could see the scars and everything. At first, all the feelings of shame and guilt came flooding back. I couldn't look him straight in the eye – how could I – I'd let him down so badly. But then he spoke to me. Words of love, words of forgiveness. I simply cannot describe how that felt.

He appeared to us again – twice – erasing any residual doubt that this incredible miracle had taken place and that this was always part of God's plan – but after that we were left with so many questions. It wasn't clear what should be happening now. Staying around in Jerusalem seemed too dangerous, so some of us went back to Galilee, where the adventure began. Lots had happened since we were last at the shore of this lake. We didn't really know what to do. We were a bit lost. Since Jesus, their leader, had been taken away from us, we felt like we'd been left like a ship without a rudder. What should we do now? No one was coming up with any decisions and I simply couldn't bear this hanging around, so I decided to do something – to go fishing. We'd been told by Jesus to wait to be clothed with power from on high; I didn't have a clue what that meant – I hate waiting for anything anyway, so I decided I was going to do something. I wanted to get on with life, and it seemed sensible to go back to the old life – after all, we all had responsibilities and families to look after, money to earn, people to feed. Catching fish seemed like a good idea. After all, that's what we were – we were fishermen. We knew the sea, we knew know where to find fish.

But, you can guess what happened next, given that this was all my brilliant idea – it didn't go to plan at all – we went out into the boat, stayed out in the water all night, but caught absolutely nothing. Not even a tiddler.

All night, no fish. Such a waste of time. We were experienced fishermen. We know that you have the best chance of catching fish in the night time. No one had told the fish that!

Now, by this time it was early morning and we had had enough. It was time to give up and go home. We were weary, and not a little bit frustrated. We were definitely ready for food and rest. We started making our way back to the shore and a man was standing there. He could probably tell the frustration we were feeling – he probably heard the grumbling coming from the boat.

He called out to us, "Friends, haven't you any fish?"

"No," we replied. Personally, I was wondering why he was asking – was he just making polite conversation?

Then he said, "Throw your net on the right side of the boat and you will find some."

On the right side of the boat? We'd been fishing off the left side all night. That's what fishermen always did. We grumbled a bit, were about to object and ask him what he knew about fishing, but something stopped us. It was John who said, "There's no harm in giving this a shot – we've got nothing to lose." I shrugged, looked around, the other blokes nodded, and so we threw the nets over to the right side of the boat as the bloke on the shore had suggested, and it was incredible! The water was teaming with fish, the net filled up – so much so that we were unable to haul the net in because there were so many fish in it.

We were looking at each other, utterly gobsmacked, exhilarated, and then John piped up, nodding his head towards the shore. "It is the Lord!"

I can't quite describe how I felt in that moment. A whole lot of things. Anxiety and guilt bubbled up in me. I had a flashback to those moments in the Garden when I struck out with my sword and then fled; those moments in the courtyard when I denied ever having known Jesus and when our gazes met before the cock crowed and I ran out weeping. I remember the disciples in Emmaus telling us that Jesus disappeared the moment they realised it was him; and part of me was hoping that he might do that again, but I looked again and he was still there, standing there on the shore, waiting for us. I could have tried to hide so I wouldn't have to face Jesus again, after all I'd let him down so badly, but I knew that wouldn't do. No, there was one thing for it.

As soon as I heard John say, "It is the Lord," I wrapped my outer garment around me and jumped into the water.

I longed to see Jesus again. We had some unfinished business to sort out. The other disciples followed close behind me, towing the net full of fish behind us.

When we landed there was a fire of burning coals there with fish on it, and some bread. Jesus had breakfast. We stood there around him, utterly dumbstruck. He smiled and said to us, "Why don't you grab some more of the fish you've just caught."

So, I climbed back into the boat and dragged the net ashore. It was full to bursting of large fish – 153 of them – we had to count that miracle catch, but even with that many the net somehow, was not torn.

Then he beckoned and said to us, "Come, sit down, join me, and have breakfast. You must be starving."

None of us dared ask him, "Who are you?" We knew it was the Lord. We sat down on the beach. He came, took the bread, and gave it to us, and did the same with the fish. It was the most wonderful breakfast we'd ever had. We were with the risen Lord Jesus who, even though going fishing was probably a stupid, impulsive idea, simply seemed to want to bless us with lots of fish and then to cook us breakfast. In that moment, whatever I'd done, I knew, somehow that it was ok, and that I was loved. And then, on that beach he gave me fresh purpose. There was no going back to the lives we had before. Jesus had changed my life forever and I knew then that all I want to do, for the rest of my life is to follow him, wherever he may take me, to fall in line with his plans and purposes for me, and that his risen presence with me and in me will make everything more than ok.

PART 2

The Power
of the Cross –
Devotional Services
for Good Friday

"Father, forgive" – A Devotional Service (based on the Gospel of Mark)[*]

[43] Just as he was speaking, Judas, one of the Twelve, appeared. With him was a crowd armed with swords and clubs, sent from the chief priests, the teachers of the law, and the elders. [44] Now the betrayer had arranged a signal with them: 'The one I kiss is the man; arrest him and lead him away under guard.' [45] Going at once to Jesus, Judas said, 'Rabbi!' and kissed him. [46] The men seized Jesus and arrested him. [47] Then one of those standing near drew his sword and struck the servant of the high priest, cutting off his ear. [48] 'Am I leading a rebellion,' said Jesus, 'that you have come out with swords and clubs to capture me? [49] Every day I was with you, teaching in the temple courts, and you did not arrest me. But the Scriptures must be fulfilled.' [50] Then everyone deserted him and fled. [51] A young man, wearing nothing but a linen garment, was following Jesus. When they seized him, [52] he fled naked, leaving his garment behind.

(Mark 14:43-52)

- - - -

Judas Iscariot – "The guilt won't let me go"

Dear Rabbi,

I'm writing this although I know it's too late. I wish I could turn back the clock, undo what I've done, but I know that there's no going back – it's past the point of no return, and there's no way I can make up for what I've done. The guilt's unbearable. I can't live with myself.

Over the time we spent together you built up our hopes that you weren't just an ordinary teacher and healer – you were

---

[*] See Appendix One for an outline of how this would fit into a traditional "Last Hour" service, including suggestions of hymns.

so much more – I knew you were going to be the one who'd bring us freedom. The crowds loved you. They would do anything for you – just one word from you and they'd join the revolution, anoint you as king, and the new era would begin. I just knew it. And then came last Sunday, when we entered the city of Jerusalem and the crowds gathered to cheer you on. You rode in on the donkey and the message was clear – you were the long-awaited king, come to take your rightful place. This was the moment we'd all been waiting for, when change would come. We, your closest friends, your disciples, we knew it; the crowds knew it too – this was the time you would come in power and we, who'd been there from the beginning – hand-picked by you, would share in your glory.

But then you did – nothing – you went back to your base that day. I thought you were biding your time, finding the right moment – perhaps the next day. And when you made that statement by clearing the temple of all that corruption and greed, I thought that would be the time, after all. But again, you did nothing. All you did was teach and debate. You had the crowds in the palm of your hand, once again, but again you bottled it. I couldn't understand why. I began to doubt – you couldn't be the king after all. Why didn't you take power? Why didn't you set us free?

Then it dawned on me. You were never intending to become king by force. You'd had more than one opportunity to seize the moment – after the mass feeding in Galilee, on that heady day in Jerusalem, in the temple, and you'd refused each one. It suddenly became clear to me   I'd been mistaken. I felt such a fool – I felt so angry – what a waste of time! All this had been for nothing. Those amazing times we had together. Those miracles, that teaching, those healings. All for nothing. I was so angry. And the problem with anger, as you yourself taught us, is that it can be deadly.

I wanted to punish you or to try and force your hand – force you to act, or do something. I'd heard the whisperings in the temple. The high priests, the authorities were out to get you – they saw what we saw, that you were a threat to their power, and the only way to deal with this threat was to get rid of you. You knew that too, and you weren't going to stop them. You were going to walk into danger and allow them to do what they wanted to you. Suddenly, I saw my chance. Chance to get my own back. I could help them, provide a way for them to get to you away from the crowd and to make some money while I was at it. Soon it was sorted out – they gleefully accepted my help. Thirty pieces of silver. Seemed like a good deal at the time. Recompense for all the disappointment. We made our plans and waited for the right moment.

And so I led them to you at the Garden, greeted you with a kiss, so they would know who you were. I'll never forget the way you looked at me. Reproachful. Sad. Hurt. Your gaze bore right into my soul and saw the darkness inside – the bitterness, the disappointment, the hurt. From a small spark, it raged like a fire in me, consumed me completely, and it led me to this. I betrayed you with a kiss. I wish I could go back, but I can't. There's no going back.

I never intended for it to end this way. I didn't really think they'd have you killed. I didn't really think you'd let them do it. They were like predators encircling their prey and they had no intention of letting you go once you were in their grasp. And you didn't fight back. Why didn't you fight back? You could have done something to show them who you really were, but instead, you let them walk over you. You let them condemn you to death. Why did you do that?

I didn't know they were going to do that! I didn't want them to do that. I only wanted them to teach you a lesson. I never meant for you to die. As soon as it dawned on me that they were going to have you killed, I realised I'd made a huge mistake. You'd done nothing to deserve any of this. You were innocent. You didn't deserve to die. You'd done nothing wrong – and I'd betrayed you. The guilt won't let me go. I will never forgive myself for what I've done.

I'm sorry. I'm so, so, sorry.

- - - -

[53] *They took Jesus to the high priest, and all the chief priests, the elders and the teachers of the law came together.* [54] *Peter followed him at a distance, right into the courtyard of the high priest. There he sat with the guards and warmed himself at the fire.*

[55] *The chief priests and the whole Sanhedrin were looking for evidence against Jesus so that they could put him to death, but they did not find any.* [56] *Many testified falsely against him, but their statements did not agree.*

[57] *Then some stood up and gave this false testimony against him:* [58] *'We heard him say, "I will destroy this temple made with human hands and in three days will build another, not made with hands."'* [59] *Yet even then their testimony did not agree.*

[60] *Then the high priest stood up before them and asked Jesus, 'Are you not going to answer? What is this testimony that these men are bringing against you?'* [61] *But Jesus remained silent and gave no answer.*

Again the high priest asked him, 'Are you the Messiah, the Son of the Blessed One?'

[62] *'I am,' said Jesus. 'And you will see the Son of Man sitting at the right hand of the Mighty One and coming on the clouds of heaven.'*

[63] *The high priest tore his clothes. 'Why do we need any more witnesses?' he asked.* [64] *'You have heard the blasphemy. What do you think?'*

They all condemned him as worthy of death. [65] *Then some began to spit at him; they blindfolded him, struck him with their fists, and said, 'Prophesy!' And the guards took him and beat him.*

[66] *While Peter was below in the courtyard, one of the servant-girls of the high priest came by.* [67] *When she saw Peter warming himself, she looked closely at him.*

'You also were with that Nazarene, Jesus,' she said.

⁶⁸ But he denied it. 'I don't know or understand what you're talking about,' he said, and went out into the entrance.
⁶⁹ When the servant-girl saw him there, she said again to those standing round them, 'This fellow is one of them.' ⁷⁰ Again he denied it.
After a little while, those standing near said to Peter, 'Surely you are one of them, for you are a Galilean.'
⁷¹ He began to call down curses, and he swore to them, 'I don't know this man you're talking about.'
⁷² Immediately the cock crowed the second time. Then Peter remembered the word Jesus had spoken to him: 'Before the cock crows twice you will disown me three times.' And he broke down and wept.

(Mark 15:53-72)

- - - -

Peter – "I let him down"

I didn't sleep a wink. I couldn't. I felt so awful. Sick in the pit of my stomach. Those words he had said to me kept going round my head. "Tonight, before the cock crows, you'll deny you've ever known me." I couldn't believe it! Me, Peter, the one he'd nicknamed Rocky, deny Jesus? I'd never deny Jesus. Never. As if I could. He was the man who had given me purpose. Life was so exciting when he was around. I'd made lots of mistakes, but he forgave every one – amazing really. How could I ever deny the man who'd turned my life upside down? Who'd allowed me to share in the greatest adventure ever? I couldn't!

But I did. Three times. Swore I didn't have the faintest idea who he was. And then he looked at me. He wasn't angry; he was reproachful. Disappointed. If I'm honest, that's worse. I was devastated. I couldn't believe I'd let Jesus down. I'd been so full of it. So full of good words and good intentions. But I couldn't back them up with my actions. I was so ashamed of myself, I ran out and wept. Wept like I've never wept before.

Friday was even worse. When Jesus needed his friends most, we deserted him – all of us, except John and some of the women in our group. It was fear that kept me away. What if they got me too and treated me the way they treated him? The one place I wanted to be was by Jesus' side – showing him that he could still depend on me and my support, yet I was too much of a coward.

So I had to rely on others to keep me posted. And the news got worse and worse as the day wore on. First, they told me that he'd been put on trial for blasphemy, that the authorities wanted his blood; then, I heard about the beating, the insults, the scourging; and then they told me he'd been sentenced to death. Crucifixion. A death so horrible that Roman citizens are spared such awful treatment. Finally, I heard the news I thought I would never hear – he'd died.

Jesus. The miracle maker. My hero. My captain. My leader. The one who was going to save us all from oppression. Dead.

I was numb. Devastated. Didn't believe it. My hopes were snuffed out with him. What was I going to do now? Where would I go?

Did you hear that I actually cut a man's ear off on Thursday night? One of the party who came to arrest Jesus. The man had it coming, if you asked me, but still, it wasn't a very clever thing to do. But Jesus healed him there and then. That's the kind of guy he was. That's why I couldn't believe that he'd died. You see, a man who could heal people in the blink of an eye. A man who could stop a storm. A man who could raise the dead. Well, that sort of man could save himself couldn't he? He couldn't be dead? So, why did he let them do that to him? Why did he let them kill him?

- - - -

¹ Very early in the morning, the chief priests, with the elders, the teachers of the law and the whole Sanhedrin, made their plans. So they bound Jesus, led him away and handed him over to Pilate.
² 'Are you the king of the Jews?' asked Pilate.
'You have said so,' Jesus replied.
³ The chief priests accused him of many things. ⁴ So again Pilate asked him, 'Aren't you going to answer? See how many things they are accusing you of.'
⁵ But Jesus still made no reply, and Pilate was amazed.
⁶ Now it was the custom at the festival to release a prisoner whom the people requested. ⁷ A man called Barabbas was in prison with the rebels who had committed murder in the uprising. ⁸ The crowd came up and asked Pilate to do for them what he usually did.
⁹ 'Do you want me to release to you the king of the Jews?' asked Pilate, ¹⁰ knowing it was out of self-interest that the chief priests had handed Jesus over to him. ¹¹ But the chief priests stirred up the crowd to get Pilate to release Barabbas instead.
¹² 'What shall I do, then, with the one you call the king of the Jews?' Pilate asked them.
¹³ 'Crucify him!' they shouted.
¹⁴ 'Why? What crime has he committed?' asked Pilate. But they shouted all the louder, 'Crucify him!'
¹⁵ Wanting to satisfy the crowd, Pilate released Barabbas to them. He had Jesus flogged, and handed him over to be crucified.
(Mark 15:1-15)

- - - -

Barabbas – "Jesus took my place"

Right now I should be dead, or dying, at least. I was involved in the uprising. The Romans call me a terrorist. I'd say I was more of a freedom fighter. The Romans deserve everything that's coming for them. Anyway, that's beside the point … the point is, I got caught and sentenced to death. I knew what that meant – the crosses are everywhere – a message to everyone that there's no messing with Rome, and soon I'd be on one. I was resigned to my fate. Nothing I could do about it.

But then, early in the morning, I was dragged out bound in front of the governor, Pilate, and the crowd. I heard something about a Jewish custom that meant a prisoner would be pardoned at Passover, and the crowd was given a choice – either I or another man, Jesus of Nazareth, could be freed. I looked over at this other man – first time I'd seen him. He certainly didn't look like your typical criminal. He was a political prisoner, apparently. Stitched up by the authorities, I reckon. Anyway, Pilate the Governor was trying to find out whose execution would be more popular – mine or his – so, here I was at the mercy of the crowd. "Who do you want me to release?" he asked, "Barabbas or Jesus who is called the Messiah?" Amazingly, the crowd cried out, "Barabbas" – my name. "And what do you want me to do with Jesus?" he asked once again. The crowd cried out, "Crucify him!" Pilate obviously smelt a rat, so he tried again. "But he's done nothing wrong." But the crowd got louder and angrier, crying out again, "Crucify him!" So Pilate washed his hands of Jesus – "his blood is on your hands," he said – and I found myself free.

I've been given my life back. Jesus took my place. There's no doubt in my mind that he's done nothing wrong, that he's an innocent man, and he took my place. I, the guilty one, have walked free. Life will be different from now on. It has to be different – I've been given a second chance. Better make the most of it.

- - - -

[16] *The soldiers led Jesus away into the palace (that is, the Praetorium) and called together the whole company of soldiers. [17] They put a purple robe on him, then twisted together a crown of thorns and set it on him. [18] And they began to call out to him, 'Hail, king of the Jews!' [19] Again and again they struck him on the head with a staff and spat on him. Falling on their knees, they paid homage to him. [20] And when they had mocked him, they took off the purple robe and put his own clothes on him. Then they led him out to crucify him.*

[21] A certain man from Cyrene, Simon, the father of Alexander and Rufus, was passing by on his way in from the country, and they forced him to carry the cross. [22] They brought Jesus to the place called Golgotha (which means 'the place of the skull'). [23] Then they offered him wine mixed with myrrh, but he did not take it. [24] And they crucified him. Dividing up his clothes, they cast lots to see what each would get. [25] It was nine in the morning when they crucified him. [26] The written notice of the charge against him read: The King of the Jews. [27] They crucified two rebels with him, one on his right and one on his left. [29] Those who passed by hurled insults at him, shaking their heads and saying, 'So! You who are going to destroy the temple and build it in three days, [30] come down from the cross and save yourself!' [31] In the same way the chief priests and the teachers of the law mocked him among themselves. 'He saved others,' they said, 'but he can't save himself! [32] Let this Messiah, this king of Israel, come down now from the cross, that we may see and believe.' Those crucified with him also heaped insults on him.

[33] At noon, darkness came over the whole land until three in the afternoon. [34] And at three in the afternoon Jesus cried out in a loud voice, 'Eloi, Eloi, lema sabachthani?' (which means 'My God, my God, why have you forsaken me?').
[35] When some of those standing near heard this, they said, 'Listen, he's calling Elijah.'

[36] Someone ran, filled a sponge with wine vinegar, put it on a staff, and offered it to Jesus to drink. 'Now leave him alone. Let's see if Elijah comes to take him down,' he said.
[37] With a loud cry, Jesus breathed his last.
[38] The curtain of the temple was torn in two from top to bottom. [39] And when the centurion, who stood there in front of Jesus, saw how he died, he said, 'Surely this man was the Son of God!'
[40] Some women were watching from a distance. Among them were Mary Magdalene, Mary the mother of James the younger and of Joseph, and Salome. [41] In Galilee these women had followed him and cared for his needs. Many other women who had come up with him to Jerusalem were also there.
[42] It was Preparation Day (that is, the day before the Sabbath). So as evening approached, [43] Joseph of Arimathea, a prominent member of the Council, who was himself waiting for the kingdom of God, went boldly to Pilate and asked for Jesus' body. [44] Pilate was surprised to hear that he was already dead. Summoning the centurion, he asked him if Jesus had already died. [45] When he learned from the centurion that it was so, he gave the body to Joseph. [46] So Joseph bought some linen cloth, took down the body, wrapped it in the linen, and placed it in a tomb cut out of rock. Then he rolled a stone against the entrance of the tomb. [47] Mary Magdalene and Mary the mother of Joseph saw where he was laid.
(Mark 15:16-47)

- - - -

Technically we should end there, with the pallor of sadness, with betrayal, sadness, hopelessness and guilt. Some of us may be in that place now – weighed down by our sin. But it wasn't the end of the story. While Judas couldn't forgive himself and thought there was no hope of redemption and forgiveness for him, Peter was given a second chance, because of what happened just two days later. Let's hear from him now …

<u>Peter – "A brand new start"</u>

Saturday dragged on. I was exhausted, but couldn't sleep; hungry, but couldn't stomach anything. A small number of Jesus' followers gathered together in secret. We cried on each other's shoulders, basically. I found out from Mary Magdalene where he'd been buried. A man called Joseph of Arimathea gave up his tomb for Jesus' body to rest. I wanted to go there, to be with Jesus one last time, but it was the Sabbath, so we couldn't go anywhere. I would have to wait until today to pay my last respects to Jesus.

But then, this morning, something extraordinary happened. Mary Magdalene came and told me that the stone blocking the entrance had been rolled away. The tomb was empty. What? Empty? How was that possible? She told me to go and see for myself. So that's what I did.

I ran to the tomb with John to check it out. To make sure that the extreme emotion we'd all experienced hadn't got to Mary's head too much. I could not believe it. She was right – the tomb was empty. I went straight into the tomb and there were the grave clothes. But no body. It had gone. Where was Jesus? Why was the tomb empty? Who moved the stone?

Could the impossible have happened? Could Jesus be alive? I could scarcely believe it. It was simply too good to be true. After all, dead men don't rise from the dead. Do they?

Later, things got even more incredible! Mary told me that she'd met with Jesus face to face – that she'd mistaken him for the gardener at first, but then she knew it was him once he'd called her by name. Perhaps it was true after all. Maybe Jesus was alive! Maybe he had defeated death!

You're not going to believe the next thing that happened! I met with him face to face! He appeared right in front of me. Out of nowhere. It was really him. I could see the scars and everything. At first, all the feelings of shame and guilt came flooding back. I couldn't look him straight in the eye – how could I – I'd let him down so badly. But then he spoke to me. He reassured me that he forgave me. That I could start over again. He told me that I was still Rocky, that I still had a part to play in the great adventure he's planned for me. In fact, he told me that there were even more incredible days ahead. He said that the adventure was only just beginning and that he would walk with me and show me the way!

Suddenly I feel more excited than ever. I can't believe that so much has happened in so little time. I can't wait to tell the other disciples that I've seen Jesus and that he's alive! Back from the dead. God is truly at work in amazing ways. Jesus is alive! He has risen! And I've been given a second chance. I can't believe it. All that guilt is gone. I'm free!

- - - -

I don't know who you identify with most this afternoon, but I think we could all do with knowing the truth that there is nothing we've thought, said or done that makes us beyond the reach of God's forgiveness. All of us are Barabbas. We are guilty, and yet Jesus, the innocent one has taken our sin, taken our shame, taken our place so we can walk free. Hear the word of the Lord:

'Come now, let us settle the matter,' says the Lord.
'Though your sins are like scarlet, they shall be as white as snow;
though they are red as crimson, they shall be like wool.
(Isaiah 1:18)

Jesus said, 'Father, forgive them, for they do not know what they are
doing.'
(Luke 23:33)

"All have sinned and fall short of the glory of God, and all are justified freely by his grace through the redemption that came by Christ Jesus."
(Romans 3:23-24)

"God demonstrates his own love for us in this: while we were still sinners, Christ died for us."
(Romans 5:8)

"God made him who had no sin to be sin for us, so that in him we might become the righteousness of God."
(2 Corinthians 5:21)

"Christ also suffered once for sins, the righteous for the unrighteous, to bring you to God."
(1 Peter 3:17-19)

"If we claim to be without sin, we deceive ourselves and the truth is not in us. If we confess our sins, God is faithful and just and will forgive us our sins and purify us from all unrighteousness."
(1 John 1:8-9)

God, the Father of mercies,
has reconciled the world to himself
through the death and resurrection of his Son, Jesus Christ,
not counting our trespasses against us,
but sending his Holy Spirit to shed abroad his love among us.
By the ministry of reconciliation
entrusted by Christ to his Church,
receive his pardon and peace
to stand before him in his strength alone,
this day and evermore. Amen.[*]

---

[*] Archbishop's Council, *Common Worship: Services and Prayers for the Church of England*, Church House Publishing (2000)

The Scandal of Grace – A Devotional Service (based on the Gospel of Luke)*

[47] *While he was still speaking a crowd came up, and the man who was called Judas, one of the Twelve, was leading them. He approached Jesus to kiss him, [48] but Jesus asked him, 'Judas, are you betraying the Son of Man with a kiss?'*

[49] When Jesus' followers saw what was going to happen, they said, 'Lord, should we strike with our swords?' [50] And one of them struck the servant of the high priest, cutting off his right ear.

[51] But Jesus answered, 'No more of this!' And he touched the man's ear and healed him.

[52] Then Jesus said to the chief priests, the officers of the temple guard, and the elders, who had come for him, 'Am I leading a rebellion, that you have come with swords and clubs? [53] Every day I was with you in the temple courts, and you did not lay a hand on me. But this is your hour – when darkness reigns.'

[54] Then seizing him, they led him away and took him into the house of the high priest. Peter followed at a distance. [55] And when some there had kindled a fire in the middle of the courtyard and had sat down together, Peter sat down with them. [56] A servant-girl saw him seated there in the firelight. She looked closely at him and said, 'This man was with him.'

[57] But he denied it. 'Woman, I don't know him,' he said.

[58] A little later someone else saw him and said, 'You also are one of them.'

'Man, I am not!' Peter replied.

[59] About an hour later another asserted, 'Certainly this fellow was with him, for he is a Galilean.'

[60] Peter replied, 'Man, I don't know what you're talking about!' Just as he was speaking, the cock crowed. [61] The Lord turned and looked straight at Peter. Then Peter remembered the word the Lord had spoken

---

* See Appendix Two for an outline of how this would fit into a traditional "Last Hour" service, including suggestions of hymns.

to him: 'Before the cock crows today, you will disown me three times.' [62] And he went outside and wept bitterly.
(Luke 22:47-62)

- - - -

<u>Peter – "I let him down"</u>

I didn't sleep a wink. I couldn't. I felt so awful. Sick in the pit of my stomach. Those words he had said to me kept going round my head. "Tonight, before the cock crows, you'll deny three times you've ever known me." I couldn't believe it! Me, Peter, the one he'd nicknamed Rocky, deny Jesus? Never. As if I could. He'd given me purpose, forgiven every one of my stupid mistakes! I excelled myself on Thursday night. Having sworn blind that I wouldn't let Jesus down, first I fell asleep in the Garden of Gethsemane when Jesus had specifically asked me to keep watch and pray with him; then, when they came to arrest Jesus, I struck out, cutting off a man's ear, even though I knew really this was the last thing Jesus would want. Didn't think, did I? Typical Jesus, he healed the man, there and then. That's the kind of guy he was. The kind of guy you follow to the very end. That's what I meant to do, at least. I followed the arresting party from Gethsemane at a distance. I wanted to be good to my word. I didn't want to abandon Jesus. Then, in the high priest's court, I didn't know what to do – Jesus had been taken off somewhere, I dread to think what they were doing to him – so I hung around and tried to remain inconspicuous. I obviously failed, because they kept looking at me suspiciously and then asked me, on three different occasions, if I had anything to do with Jesus. Each time, I said no. Each denial was a kick to the stomach. The final time, the cock crowed. Jesus turned and looked at me. Despite my bold and brash words, despite my good intentions, it'd all happened as Jesus had said it would. He'd probably even heard my final denial. Just imagine how he must have felt in that moment; me, his Rock, his closest friend, denied knowing him. His look wasn't one of anger. Actually, believe it or not, it was a look of love. Forgiveness, even. Well, I couldn't handle that. I'd let Jesus down. I was so ashamed of myself, I ran out and wept. Wept like I've never wept before. How could I have denied the man who'd turned my life upside down? Who'd allowed me to share in the greatest adventure ever? I couldn't! And yet I did. I let Jesus down. Lord, please forgive me.

Prayer:

Confess to God any areas where you feel you have let him down.

- - - -

⁶³ The men who were guarding Jesus began mocking and beating him. ⁶⁴ They blindfolded him and demanded, 'Prophesy! Who hit you?' ⁶⁵ And they said many other insulting things to him.

⁶⁶ At daybreak the council of the elders of the people, both the chief priests and the teachers of the law, met together, and Jesus was led before them. ⁶⁷ 'If you are the Messiah,' they said, 'tell us.'
Jesus answered, 'If I tell you, you will not believe me, ⁶⁸ and if I asked you, you would not answer. ⁶⁹ But from now on, the Son of Man will be seated at the right hand of the mighty God.'
⁷⁰ They all asked, 'Are you then the Son of God?'
He replied, 'You say that I am.'
⁷¹ Then they said, 'Why do we need any more testimony? We have heard it from his own lips.'
23 Then the whole assembly rose and led him off to Pilate. ² And they began to accuse him, saying, 'We have found this man subverting our nation. He opposes payment of taxes to Caesar and claims to be Messiah, a king.'

3 So Pilate asked Jesus, 'Are you the king of the Jews?'
'You have said so,' Jesus replied.
4 Then Pilate announced to the chief priests and the crowd, 'I find no basis for a charge against this man.'
5 But they insisted, 'He stirs up the people all over Judea by his teaching. He started in Galilee and has come all the way here.'
6 On hearing this, Pilate asked if the man was a Galilean. 7 When he learned that Jesus was under Herod's jurisdiction, he sent him to Herod, who was also in Jerusalem at that time.
8 When Herod saw Jesus, he was greatly pleased, because for a long time he had been wanting to see him. From what he had heard about him, he hoped to see him perform a sign of some sort. 9 He plied him with many questions, but Jesus gave him no answer. 10 The chief priests and the teachers of the law were standing there, vehemently accusing him. 11 Then Herod and his soldiers ridiculed and mocked him. Dressing him in an elegant robe, they sent him back to Pilate. 12 That day Herod and Pilate became friends – before this they had been enemies.
13 Pilate called together the chief priests, the rulers and the people, 14 and said to them, 'You brought me this man as one who was inciting the people to rebellion. I have examined him in your presence and have found no basis for your charges against him. 15 Neither has Herod, for he sent him back to us; as you can see, he has done nothing to deserve death. 16 Therefore, I will punish him and then release him.' [a]
18 But the whole crowd shouted, 'Away with this man! Release Barabbas to us!' 19 (Barabbas had been thrown into prison for an insurrection in the city, and for murder.)
20 Wanting to release Jesus, Pilate appealed to them again. 21 But they kept shouting, 'Crucify him! Crucify him!'
22 For the third time he spoke to them: 'Why? What crime has this man committed? I have found in him no grounds for the death penalty. Therefore I will have him punished and then release him.'
23 But with loud shouts they insistently demanded that he be crucified, and their shouts prevailed. 24 So Pilate decided to grant their demand. 25 He released the man who had been thrown into prison for

insurrection and murder, the one they asked for, and surrendered Jesus
to their will.
(Luke 22:63 – 23:25)

- - - -

Barabbas – "Jesus took my place"

Right now, I should be dead, or dying, at least. I was involved in the uprising. The Romans call me a terrorist. I'd say I was more of a freedom fighter. The Romans deserve everything that's coming for them. Anyway, that's beside the point … the point is, I got caught and sentenced to death. I knew what that meant – the crosses are everywhere – a message to everyone that there's no messing with Rome, and soon I'd be on one. I was resigned to my fate. Nothing I could do about it.

But then, early in the morning, I was dragged out bound in front of the governor, Pilate, and the crowd. I heard something about a Jewish custom that meant a prisoner would be pardoned at Passover, and the crowd was given a choice – either I or another man, Jesus of Nazareth, could be freed. I looked over at this other man – first time I'd seen him. He certainly didn't look like your typical criminal. He was a political prisoner, apparently. Stitched up by the authorities, I reckon. Anyway, Pilate the Governor was trying to find out whose execution would be more popular – mine or his – so, here I was at the mercy of the crowd. "Who do you want me to release?" he asked, "Barabbas or Jesus who is called the Messiah?" Amazingly, the crowd cried out, "Barabbas" – my name. "And what do you want me to do with Jesus?" he asked once again. The crowd cried out, "Crucify him!" Pilate obviously smelt a rat, so he tried again. "But he's done nothing wrong." But the crowd got louder and angrier, crying out again, "Crucify him!" So Pilate gave in, and I found myself free.

I've been given my life back. Jesus took my place. There's no doubt in my mind that he's done nothing wrong, that he's an innocent man, and he took my place. I, the guilty one, have walked free. Life will be different from now on. It has to be different – I've been given a second chance. Better make the most of it.

Prayer:

Give thanks that Jesus gives each of us a second chance.

- - - -

26 As the soldiers led him away, they seized Simon from Cyrene, who was on his way in from the country, and put the cross on him and made him carry it behind Jesus. 27 A large number of people followed him, including women who mourned and wailed for him. 28 Jesus turned and said to them, 'Daughters of Jerusalem, do not weep for me; weep for yourselves and for your children. 29 For the time will come when you will say, "Blessed are the childless women, the wombs that never bore and the breasts that never nursed!" 30 Then

*"'they will say to the mountains, "Fall on us!"
and to the hills, "Cover us!"'*

31 For if people do these things when the tree is green, what will happen when it is dry?'

32 Two other men, both criminals, were also led out with him to be executed. 33 When they came to the place called the Skull, they crucified him there, along with the criminals – one on his right, the other on his left. 34 Jesus said, 'Father, forgive them, for they do not know what they are doing.'[g] And they divided up his clothes by casting lots.

35 The people stood watching, and the rulers even sneered at him. They said, 'He saved others; let him save himself if he is God's Messiah, the Chosen One.'

³⁶ The soldiers also came up and mocked him. They offered him wine vinegar ³⁷ and said, 'If you are the king of the Jews, save yourself.'
³⁸ There was a written notice above him, which read: this is the king of the Jews.
³⁹ One of the criminals who hung there hurled insults at him: 'Aren't you the Messiah? Save yourself and us!'
⁴⁰ But the other criminal rebuked him. 'Don't you fear God,' he said, 'since you are under the same sentence? ⁴¹ We are punished justly, for we are getting what our deeds deserve. But this man has done nothing wrong.'
⁴² Then he said, 'Jesus, remember me when you come into your kingdom.[d] '
⁴³ Jesus answered him, 'Truly I tell you, today you will be with me in paradise.'
(Luke 23:26-43)

- - - -

A Thief in Paradise

I'm not a good man. I've done some horrible things. I've stolen, hurt people, I even killed someone. I never intended that, it kind of happened. Anyway, I got caught and sentenced to death. I deserved it – deserved everything that came to me.

Three of us were up on those crosses being crucified that day. One was like me – a robber – a bandit, getting his just desserts, just like me. The other one, Jesus, was different – he just seemed innocent, a victim of some horrendous injustice.

Crucifixion is awful. The beatings are bad enough, but then they nail you to that cross. While we were being nailed, me and this other robber bloke were swearing and cursing, wishing we'd never been born. Jesus at first, didn't say a word, but then he did. It was amazing. "Father, forgive them," he said, "They don't know what they're doing." How can he say that? He was innocent; it was a disgrace the way they'd treated

74

him. Yet, he could ask God to forgive them? They didn't deserve it, they deserved to be punished, just like us. And yet he forgave them. That's incredible.

Anyway, this man had to put up with being mocked and spat on. Again, he said nothing, took it all on the chin. Didn't get bitter or angry. And then the other guy started joining in. He sneered at Jesus, "if you're who you say you are, why don't you save us and yourself. As if you could."

I'd kept my mouth shut until then, but I couldn't stand it any more – how could they do this to this bloke. He'd done nothing wrong! I turned to the other thief and said, "don't you fear God? You should do! You and I are guilty as sin. We've paid the price, we deserve to be here. But this man has done nothing wrong! He's innocent. Just leave him alone."

I don't know why I said the next bit, but something in him gave me hope – hope for someone like me. So, I turned to Jesus and said, "Jesus, remember me when you come into your kingdom." I knew he was a King, but not the usual sort of King. And I knew he was the only hope that I could possibly have. I wasn't expecting much; I didn't deserve much good to happen to me – I was expecting him to reject me like everyone else had.

But he said something incredible; something I will never forget and always be thankful for. He turned to me and said, "Today you'll be with me in paradise."

Me, a crook, a murderer, a scumbag, an awful, awful man, in paradise. I don't deserve it. I don't deserve to be loved in such a way. And yet, here I am. A thief in paradise. – and it's amazing. Why am I here? Because a crucified King opened the door and let me in. There is hope for people even like me – and it's amazing!

Prayer:

Give thanks for the hope of heaven for those who have faith
in Jesus' power to save.

- - - -

*⁴⁴ It was now about noon, and darkness came over the whole land until
three in the afternoon, ⁴⁵ for the sun stopped shining. And the curtain of
the temple was torn in two. ⁴⁶ Jesus called out with a loud voice, 'Father,
into your hands I commit my spirit.' When he had said this, he
breathed his last.*
*⁴⁷ The centurion, seeing what had happened, praised God and said,
'Surely this was a righteous man.' ⁴⁸ When all the people who had
gathered to witness this sight saw what took place, they beat their breasts
and went away. ⁴⁹ But all those who knew him, including the women
who had followed him from Galilee, stood at a distance, watching these
things.*

(Luke 23:44-49)

- - - -

The Centurion – "Could I be forgiven too?"

It's my job as a centurion to keep the peace. Not an easy task
at Jewish festival season. Hundreds of thousands of people
flock from all over the country for their celebrations – and
there's almost always trouble. We know it's coming now –
we're used to snuffing out any rebellion before it has any
chance of getting going. The ringleaders are arrested, whipped
and then crucified. This generally nips the trouble in the bud.

We crucified three that day. Two were pretty standard –
they were bandits and murderers, but there was something
different about the third man. He was different – an apparent
rebel, sentenced to death on the insistence of the local rulers,
who wanted rid of him no matter what and promised our

Governor Pilate trouble if he didn't give in. Seemed very fishy to me.

When he was handed over to us, we led him out to Skull Hill, just outside the city. He was too weak to carry the cross himself, so we got someone from the crowd to carry it for him. And we crucified him – with those two bandits. When he was up there, people hurled insults on him.

Normally our victims shout and scream and curse, but he didn't. He said very little. And the words he did say will be words I'll never forget. As we were nailing him to the cross, he managed to say, "Father, forgive them. They don't what they're doing." Wow. I didn't think much of it then, but the more I think of it, the more it amazes me. Here was a man who was innocent, who'd been brutally treated and mocked, and crucified, uttering words of forgiveness to the very people who'd put him there.

At about noon, something really strange happened – the sky went pitch black. It was spooky. Somehow, I knew that this darkness was to do with Jesus. Something was going on that was bigger than the death of a common criminal. It stayed dark for about three hours, and then Jesus gave a loud cry, calling out to his God, "Father, into your hands I commit my spirit.' He'd obviously come to a place of peace. Those were the last words he said, as he died soon afterwards.

I'd watched him all that day. He'd gone through such unimaginable horror, and yet never once did he rise to bitterness or anger. Amazing! I've watched many men die, and I can tell you there was something different about him. He was no ordinary criminal, no ordinary man. I knew he was special, so I cried out, "Surely, he was a righteous man."

"Father, forgive them," he said. "Father, forgive them." God knows the terrible things I've done; the blood on my hands. I don't deserve to be forgiven, and yet that man, Jesus, forgave all those who killed him. That includes me. Could it be that I've been forgiven too? That all the terrible things I've done in my life have been wiped away? Could it be that I can have a brand new start, that these bloodied hands might be able to be clean once more?

Prayer:

Are there any areas of life where you feel like you need a brand new start? Commit them to Jesus.

- - - -

[50] Now there was a man named Joseph, a member of the Council, a good and upright man, [51] who had not consented to their decision and action. He came from the Judean town of Arimathea, and he himself was waiting for the kingdom of God. [52] Going to Pilate, he asked for Jesus' body. [53] Then he took it down, wrapped it in linen cloth and placed it in a tomb cut in the rock, one in which no one had yet been laid. [54] It was Preparation Day, and the Sabbath was about to begin. [55] The women who had come with Jesus from Galilee followed Joseph and saw the tomb and how his body was laid in it. [56] Then they went home and prepared spices and perfumes. But they rested on the Sabbath in obedience to the commandment.

(Luke 23:50-56)

- - - -

Joseph of Arimathea – Out of the shadows

I'll never forget the first time I saw Jesus. He was teaching in the temple courts. There was something compelling about the way he spoke, telling his hearers about the Kingdom of God. I long to see God's kingdom come. I long to see justice and mercy, to see desperate people finding hope and healing, as the prophets foretold. Then, when I heard Jesus speak and saw the things he did, it dawned on me that the Kingdom of God was coming through him. He was the one about whom the prophets had spoken. But not everyone saw it that way. I'm part of the Sanhedrin, the temple council; we advise the High Priest. Most of us try and make decisions that uphold our faith and honour the Lord, but others see it as a means to power. Well, over time, it became clear that the high priest and some others saw Jesus as a threat. At first, they viewed him as an irritant, but the more he spoke up and challenged their hypocrisy, the more popular he seemed to get with the people, the more determined the High Priest and some of the Sanhedrin were to have Jesus silenced. This all came to a head in the week leading to the Passover. Throughout the week, he was very open in his criticism of the temple authorities and from the mutterings I'd heard, it was clear they'd had enough of him. This teacher had to go.

I wasn't there at his trial. I'm not important enough. Caiaphas, the high priest had organised it without me, assembled enough of his supporters to ensure they could pass a death sentence – they only needed twenty-three to get the job done. Though I'd kept quiet about my allegiance to Jesus, Caiaphas would have known I wasn't going to be in cahoots with his plans. I was horrified when I found out what had happened. They'd sentenced an innocent man to death. I did not consent to this decision. I played no part in this action. It made me ashamed to be part of such a council and never to have spoken up for this man.

During that awful day, when Jesus was dying on that cross, I wanted to help him somehow, to do something to show where my allegiance truly lay, but I couldn't think what. Then, when I heard that Jesus had died, I knew what I could do. I went to Pilate and obtained his permission to bury Jesus and place him in the tomb that had just been dug for myself and my family. We bought the grave clothes, had Jesus taken down from the cross, wrapped up his body and placed it in the tomb. Everyone else on the council was now busy getting ready for the Passover, they weren't going to pose an immediate danger to me, but in time everyone will find out where my allegiance really lies, that I'm a follower of Jesus of Nazareth, who was wrongly killed today. They will find out in time, and I'm not afraid of what they might do to me. It's time to step out of the shadows. It's time to be counted.

Prayer:

Pray for courage to step out of the shadows and make it known that you are a follower of Jesus.

Faith, hope, and courage –
A Devotional Service
(based on the Gospel of John)[*]

²⁸ Then the Jewish leaders took Jesus from Caiaphas to the palace of the Roman governor. By now it was early morning, and to avoid ceremonial uncleanness they did not enter the palace, because they wanted to be able to eat the Passover. ²⁹ So Pilate came out to them and asked, "What charges are you bringing against this man?"

³⁰ "If he were not a criminal," they replied, "we would not have handed him over to you."

³¹ Pilate said, "Take him yourselves and judge him by your own law." "But we have no right to execute anyone," they objected. ³² This took place to fulfil what Jesus had said about the kind of death he was going to die.

³³ Pilate then went back inside the palace, summoned Jesus and asked him, "Are you the king of the Jews?"

³⁴ "Is that your own idea," Jesus asked, "or did others talk to you about me?"

³⁵ "Am I a Jew?" Pilate replied. "Your own people and chief priests handed you over to me. What is it you have done?"

³⁶ Jesus said, "My kingdom is not of this world. If it were, my servants would fight to prevent my arrest by the Jewish leaders. But now my kingdom is from another place."

³⁷ "You are a king, then!" said Pilate.

Jesus answered, "You say that I am a king. In fact, the reason I was born and came into the world is to testify to the truth. Everyone on the side of truth listens to me."

³⁸ "What is truth?" retorted Pilate. With this he went out again to the Jews gathered there and said, "I find no basis for a charge against him. ³⁹ But it is your custom for me to release to you one prisoner at the time of the Passover. Do you want me to release 'the king of the Jews'?"

---

[*] See Appendix Three for an outline of how this would fit into a traditional "Last Hour" service, including suggestions of hymns.

⁴⁰ They shouted back, "No, not him! Give us Barabbas!" Now Barabbas had taken part in an uprising.
(John 18:28-40)

- - - -

Pontius Pilate – The Blame Game (1)

He really ruined my day, you know. All was going well in Jerusalem until he came along. I was doing my bit, keeping law and order – which isn't easy to do with that riff-raff, especially when it's their festival season. I don't know what they put in the water, but everyone seems to get rather excited. Tempers flare up and before you know it, you have a full-blown riot on your hands – and you can't have that. The walls have ears you know, and any hint that you've lost control, Caesar is sure to find out, and then there'll be trouble. No, it needs a steady hand to keep the peace, you know: A man of intelligence, experience, courage; a master diplomat; a man of the people. Someone exactly like me, in fact.

And that's what I was doing that Friday morning: keeping the peace. The religious authorities – who, by the way, are far too big for their boots – called on me to intervene in their affairs. A man, Jesus, from the north, was causing them trouble. I couldn't quite see what the fuss was all about; couldn't they deal with the problem themselves? After all, this man was their problem, wasn't he? But they insisted, saying he was calling himself the King of the Jews, and that only I had the authority to execute the man. So, I interviewed him; and quite frankly I couldn't see any reason to charge him of any crime. He talked about having a kingdom from another place. He said that he came to testify to truth. All in all, he wasn't a threat to anyone. So I made up my mind: I was going to release him. No one was going to push me around.

- - - -

¹ Then Pilate took Jesus and had him flogged. ² The soldiers twisted together a crown of thorns and put it on his head. They clothed him in a purple robe ³ and went up to him again and again, saying, "Hail, king of the Jews!" And they slapped him in the face.

⁴ Once more Pilate came out and said to the Jews gathered there, "Look, I am bringing him out to you to let you know that I find no basis for a charge against him." ⁵ When Jesus came out wearing the crown of thorns and the purple robe, Pilate said to them, "Here is the man!"

⁶ As soon as the chief priests and their officials saw him, they shouted, "Crucify! Crucify!"

But Pilate answered, "You take him and crucify him. As for me, I find no basis for a charge against him."

⁷ The Jewish leaders insisted, "We have a law, and according to that law he must die, because he claimed to be the Son of God."

⁸ When Pilate heard this, he was even more afraid, ⁹ and he went back inside the palace. "Where do you come from?" he asked Jesus, but Jesus gave him no answer. ¹⁰ "Do you refuse to speak to me?" Pilate said. "Don't you realize I have power either to free you or to crucify you?"

¹¹ Jesus answered, "You would have no power over me if it were not given to you from above. Therefore the one who handed me over to you is guilty of a greater sin."

¹² From then on, Pilate tried to set Jesus free, but the Jewish leaders kept shouting, "If you let this man go, you are no friend of Caesar. Anyone who claims to be a king opposes Caesar."

¹³ When Pilate heard this, he brought Jesus out and sat down on the judge's seat at a place known as the Stone Pavement (which in Aramaic is Gabbatha). ¹⁴ It was the day of Preparation of the Passover; it was about noon.

"Here is your king," Pilate said to the Jews.

¹⁵ But they shouted, "Take him away! Take him away! Crucify him!"

"Shall I crucify your king?" Pilate asked.

"We have no king but Caesar," the chief priests answered.
[16] *Finally Pilate handed him over to them to be crucified.*
(John 19:1-16)

- - - -

Pontius Pilate – The Blame Game (2)

I'm here to keep the peace, you know. I'm very good at it, actually. Every decision I make is in the interest of keeping the peace. That Jesus was simply causing too much trouble. The Jewish leaders didn't want him around anymore. I told him I was trying to help him, but he wasn't at all cooperative! In fact, he said that the only reason I have any power at all is because it's been given to me from above. The cheek of it! I'm a very powerful man, and what I say goes in this part of the world. But those Jewish leaders kept on nagging and nagging; they just wouldn't shut up. So, I gave in and handed him over so they could do what they wanted with this man. I only did it to keep the peace; so why can't I find any peace myself?

I mean, I had the best of intentions. It was obvious to me that he was innocent. I did my best to let him off. It's not my fault he's dead. It's not my fault. All I'm trying to do is keep the peace. To do my job. I don't think any one else would have done better in my position. I had the best of intentions. It's not my fault that it didn't work out exactly as I'd planned, is it? If you want to blame anyone, blame the Jewish leaders – they were the ones who wanted him dead. There would have been all-out rebellion had they not got their way. I only backed down to keep the peace; so why can't I find any peace myself?

Prayer/reflection:

How often do we seek to justify ourselves and blame other
people when things go wrong?
Reflect on this with God and ask for his forgiveness.

*Lord, forgive us for blaming others for things that go wrong. Help us to
take responsibility for our actions. Forgive us, we pray, and cleanse us
from our guilt.*

- - - -

So the soldiers took charge of Jesus. [17] *Carrying his own cross, he went
out to the place of the Skull (which in Aramaic is called Golgotha).* [18]
*There they crucified him, and with him two others—one on each side
and Jesus in the middle.*
[19] *Pilate had a notice prepared and fastened to the cross. It read:
JESUS OF NAZARETH, THE KING OF THE JEWS.* [20]
*Many of the Jews read this sign, for the place where Jesus was crucified
was near the city, and the sign was written in Aramaic, Latin and
Greek.* [21] *The chief priests of the Jews protested to Pilate, "Do not write
'The King of the Jews,' but that this man claimed to be king of the
Jews."*
[22] *Pilate answered, "What I have written, I have written."*
[23] *When the soldiers crucified Jesus, they took his clothes, dividing them
into four shares, one for each of them, with the undergarment remaining.
This garment was seamless, woven in one piece from top to bottom.*
[24] *"Let's not tear it," they said to one another. "Let's decide by lot who
will get it."*
*This happened that the scripture might be fulfilled that said,
"They divided my clothes among them
and cast lots for my garment."
So this is what the soldiers did.*
[25] *Near the cross of Jesus stood his mother, his mother's sister, Mary the
wife of Clopas, and Mary Magdalene.* [26] *When Jesus saw his mother
there, and the disciple whom he loved standing nearby, he said to her,*

"Woman, here is your son," [27] *and to the disciple, "Here is your mother." From that time on, this disciple took her into his home.*
(John 19:16-27)

- - - -

Mary – Sunshine and Shadows

I watched him die. There was nothing I could do about it. There is nothing worse than seeing your child die in any circumstances, but the way he died made it even worse. He'd been beaten and whipped so badly that I barely recognised him. The agony was etched across his face. It was just so cruel. And there was absolutely nothing I could do about it. I was helpless. It's a mother's duty to look after her son, but I just stood there, powerless, as his life ebbed slowly away.

To add insult to injury, the soldiers and passers-by mocked him. The soldiers even gambled for his clothing while he was nailed to that cross, dying. I wanted to shout at them, to stop them, to ask them to help my son, or at least ease his suffering in some way, instead of acting as if he was there for their enjoyment. It broke my heart.

And as he hanged there dying, flashbacks came to me of moments that I treasured throughout his life. The moment I first held him and wrapped him in those swaddling bands to protect him from the cold, Bethlehem night; those extraordinary visitors we had when he was born; the first smile; his strange disappearance in Jerusalem; the day he first worked with Joseph in the workshop; the day he told me he was beginning his ministry of teaching and healing. The way he spoke to me, it was clear he was saying goodbye. He knew his message would get him into trouble with the religious and political leaders: I think he knew that they would end up killing him; but it didn't stop him. Nothing would stop him from carrying out God's will. And now his journey has ended here;

86

his life in the hands of people who have nothing but hate in their eyes.

He could have complained. He could have given in to self-pity or anger – and would have been perfectly within his rights to do so. After all, he didn't deserve what was happening to him – it was so *unfair*! And yet, he was selfless, as usual, thinking of others before himself. He looked at me, and our friend, John, and made sure that I'd be looked after. My dear, dear, son, looking after my interests, when I should be the one looking after him. But out of the deep, deep hurt, healing has come. And he did often say that he would rise again on the third day. Is it foolish to believe that this isn't the end? Is it possible that out of the darkness, light will come? Jesus has brought hope to so many people. Is it foolish to believe that there is still reason to hope?

Prayer/reflection:

Where has your heart been broken? Have there been times when it's been tempting to lose hope? Where do you need God's healing touch?

Living Lord, you bring hope out of hopelessness, light out of darkness, and healing out of hurt. Please come in your power to minister to our brokenness and pain. Amen.

- - - -

[28] *Later, knowing that everything had now been finished, and so that Scripture would be fulfilled, Jesus said, "I am thirsty."* [29] *A jar of wine vinegar was there, so they soaked a sponge in it, put the sponge on a stalk of the hyssop plant, and lifted it to Jesus' lips.* [30] *When he had received the drink, Jesus said, "It is finished." With that, he bowed his head and gave up his spirit.*
[31] *Now it was the day of Preparation, and the next day was to be a special Sabbath. Because the Jewish leaders did not want the bodies left*

on the crosses during the Sabbath, they asked Pilate to have the legs broken and the bodies taken down. [32] The soldiers therefore came and broke the legs of the first man who had been crucified with Jesus, and then those of the other. [33] But when they came to Jesus and found that he was already dead, they did not break his legs. [34] Instead, one of the soldiers pierced Jesus' side with a spear, bringing a sudden flow of blood and water. [35] The man who saw it has given testimony, and his testimony is true. He knows that he tells the truth, and he testifies so that you also may believe. [36] These things happened so that the scripture would be fulfilled: "Not one of his bones will be broken," [37] and, as another scripture says, "They will look on the one they have pierced."

[38] Later, Joseph of Arimathea asked Pilate for the body of Jesus. Now Joseph was a disciple of Jesus, but secretly because he feared the Jewish leaders. With Pilate's permission, he came and took the body away. [39] He was accompanied by Nicodemus, the man who earlier had visited Jesus at night. Nicodemus brought a mixture of myrrh and aloes, about seventy-five pounds. [40] Taking Jesus' body, the two of them wrapped it, with the spices, in strips of linen. This was in accordance with Jewish burial customs. [41] At the place where Jesus was crucified, there was a garden, and in the garden a new tomb, in which no one had ever been laid. [42] Because it was the Jewish day of Preparation and since the tomb was nearby, they laid Jesus there.

(John 19:28-42)

- - - -

Nicodemus – No longer afraid

The first time I met him face-to-face was in the middle of the night. I'd seen him at a distance before; been there when he'd engaged in debates with the other religious leaders. He was extraordinary. Whenever he spoke, something burned within me. He also performed the most incredible miracles – healing the sick, turning water into wine – that only someone inspired by God could do. I had to come and see him. I had to find out more about him. The problem was that I was rather important – I had a place on the Jewish ruling council – and I didn't want others to find out I'd met with him. They were threatened by him, you see. So, I came to see him in the middle of the night, so I wouldn't lose face.

I'll never forget that encounter. He spoke about the need to be born again and said that we could have eternal life if we believed in him. At first, I didn't have a clue what he was talking about, it seemed so new, so confusing. I didn't sleep for days afterwards. I didn't know it at the time, but my heart was beginning to change. I found myself sticking up for him when the Pharisees began to criticise him. They felt threatened by what they'd heard about Jesus, so refused to allow themselves to actually listen to what he was saying. I may have done that once, but no more.

I could scarcely believe the events of this past week. I knew they'd got it in for him, especially after Lazarus was raised from the dead, but I didn't really think that they would succeed in having him executed. I was there at his trial. I watched, helpless, in horror as they levelled groundless accusations at him and contrived to have him sentenced to death. I wish I could have spoken out, but I was frightened. They could have turned on me. So I kept silent. Not any more. It's time to step out of the shadows. It's time to stand up and be counted; to show that I'm not afraid any more – not afraid to be identified as his follower. That's why I went with Joseph of Arimathea – another one who had been afraid to speak out – to make sure Jesus got a proper burial. It's the least I can do for him. And now everyone knows where my allegiance lies. And I don't care what they do to me. I don't know what the future holds, but I do know that I feel like there's new life coursing through my veins and I feel more alive than ever. Perhaps that's what Jesus meant when he spoke about being born again!

Prayer/reflection:

How prepared are we to show that we're not afraid of following Jesus and being identified with him?

Risen Lord Jesus, forgive us for when we've been afraid to be known as your followers. Please give us boldness to make Jesus known through our words and actions and to give our all to you. Amen.

PART 3
Proclaiming Hope – The Message of Holy Week and Easter

Two Kingdoms – Palm Sunday – Matthew 21:1-11)

Today we celebrate Jesus' entry into Jerusalem on Palm Sunday, when he came from the East and was welcomed as King by the people. It was Jesus' triumphal entry. Another man entered the city that day and had his own triumphal entry. He was Pontius Pilate, and he represented a completely different kingdom. He came from the West. Let's hear about these two men and their two kingdoms.

A: He's coming from the West.

B: He's coming from the East

A: In a mighty procession of gleaming armour and burnished leather

B: There's no armour, no weapons, just a man in flowing robes

A: Warriors on horseback lead the way

B: He's riding a donkey

A: The crowd is beaten and pushed out of the way

B: The crowd is welcomed

A: The people are fearful – they cower and flee

B: The people are joyous – they lay their cloaks on the ground, and cut branches and lie them before him

A: The people are silent

B: The people cry out – Blessed is he who comes in the name of the Lord

A: The message is clear.

B: The message is clear.

A: The Emperor's representative has come

B: The King has come

A: He's come to take charge

B: He's come to set people free

A: He's come for those who are powerful and important.

B: He's come for everybody
A: No wonder people are afraid
B: No wonder people love him.
A: It's a kingdom of power and prestige, grandeur, political and military authority
B: It's a kingdom of compassion, humility, love, suffering; but most of all, peace.
A: You can't live in both.
B: Which one will you choose?

- - - -

Yesterday evening a great battle was fought in London. It was a battle so important that it split a city, communities, families in two. In the streets of a certain city, neutrality was impossible. You were either red or blue. It was of course the FA Cup semi-final between the two main clubs of Manchester – United and City. In Manchester you would have to make a choice. City or United. Whose side were you on? Here, of course, you're either Vale or Stoke. There is no room for neutrals. Whose side are you on?

Let's go back to Jerusalem, 2,000 years ago. It's the beginning of Passover week – the most important week in the Jewish calendar – and the city is engulfed in a sea of pilgrims. Those who can afford it, or have friends or relatives living there stay in the city itself. Thousands others form tent cities outside the city walls. Into this mass of people come two very different processions, representing two different kingdoms. From the West, Pontius Pilate comes in a procession of gleaming armour, burnished leather, cavalrymen on horseback and the imperial eagle on standard leading the procession. Foot soldiers beat and push the populace out of the way. This is a display of power, letting the city know that the emperor's representative is marching in to take charge of the city.

From the East, a man makes his own triumphal entry. This entry has been just as well planned. This entry is making an equally strong statement. But it's very different. No armour, no swords are in sight. Instead of warhorses, there is a donkey ridden by a man in flowing robes. The crowd is raucous, joyful. They treat him as royalty, throwing their cloaks before him, and cutting off palm branches and lying them on the road too.

Men and women of all backgrounds gather to acclaim this man, shouting

"Hosanna to the Son of David!"

"Blessed is he who comes in the name of the Lord!"

"Hosanna in the highest heaven!"

The message is clear to all in Jerusalem. The King has come. Some acclaim him, because he has changed their lives through his preaching, his healing, his compassion. Others are there because they are tired of oppression and long for freedom – they see that this man could be the answer to their prayers.

So, into Jerusalem on that heady day, two kingdoms converge. One of power and prestige, grandeur, political and military authority – the Kingdom of the world, which seems so enticing, that seems to offer so much. The other kingdom is a kingdom of compassion, humility, love, suffering; but most of all, peace. A kingdom that seems superficially to offer so little, but that offers the most precious thing of all: eternal security, eternal peace between humanity and God. In the words of the old western cliché, the town wasn't big enough for these two kingdoms. There was no room for neutrality, there was no sitting on the fence. You had to make a choice – do you choose Jesus' kingdom or the kingdom of the world? This was the choice that Jesus presented to the people that day: to the leaders of the temple, to the scribes and the lawmakers and the temple police, to the pilgrims in their tents and the poor in their tenements – and to everyone who has sought to follow him ever since: which king are you going to choose? The rule of Rome or the kingdom of God? Whose side are you on?

Jesus asks us the same question today. Whose side are we on? Do we choose the world, and receive the instant but empty rewards on offer, or do we choose Jesus and inherit the eternal rewards he offers? And how do our lives match up to the choices we've made? How far do our lives demonstrate that we're following the Prince of Peace, who brought such love, compassion, and transformation to people's lives? Are we people who others see as being characterised by compassion and love? Is there something different about us? Where do we find our security? God help us to live lives worthy of our King.

The Feast – Mark 14:12-25

I love feasting, don't you? Feasting seems so appropriate at significant moments of our lives. We enjoy eating together, don't we?

Jesus loved feasting too – so much so that he was criticized for being a glutton and hanging out with so-called "sinners". In the Gospels we see him eating with all sorts of people, enjoying their company, showing them how much they are valued by spending time with them. This morning, we come to look at that most famous of feasts – the Last Supper.

We're so familiar with it, aren't we? We recount this story and these events every week, and yet again, there is a danger that we forget the mystery, the danger, the sadness of this particular evening. Let's imagine we're hearing this for the first time, or, even better, imagine we are one of the disciples in the upper room, watching our Lord take bread and wine.

So, let's look at this passage together – Mark 14:12-25 – and let's allow it to come to life.

The first thing that's important to know is that we are approaching arguably the most important of Jewish festivals, Passover. Thousands, even hundreds of thousands of pilgrims would throng the city to celebrate – what, exactly?

In short, the Passover celebration – seder – that is still celebrated by Jews today is an annual meal celebrating and commemorating a defining moment in Israel's history. Jews remember when God acted decisively to rescue the Israelites from hundreds of years of slavery in Egypt. God heard their cries and intervened, commanding Moses to confront Pharoah and tell him, in no uncertain terms, to "let my people go." So Moses went to Pharoah, who refused categorically. Then in a series of incredibly dramatic chapters in Exodus, we see a battle between Moses and Pharaoh. As a punishment for

Pharaoh's hardheartedness, ten plagues were inflicted on Egypt, resulting in the poisoning of the water, death of livestock, destruction of crops, and so on. With each plague Pharaoh refused to budge – he wouldn't let the people go - until finally, it came to the final plague. A plague of death. Moses came to Pharaoh one last time – if you don't let my people go, the firstborn son of every Egyptian – from the Pharaoh to the slaves – will die. Again, Pharaoh refused to listen, and in Timothy Keller's words,

> God sent the final plague; he unsheathed the sword of divine justice. And this justice would fall on everyone. It could not "pass over" the Jews simply because they were Jews. In every home in Egypt—of Jews and Egyptians alike—someone would die under the wrath of justice. The only way for your family to escape was to put your faith in God's sacrificial provision; namely, you had to slay a lamb and put the blood on the doors as a sign of your faith in God. In every home that night there would either be a dead child or a dead lamb. When justice came down, either it fell on your family or you took shelter under the substitute, under the blood of the lamb. If you did accept this shelter, then death passed over you and you were saved; that's why it was called Passover. You were saved only on the basis of faith in a substitutionary sacrifice. This is how God delivered the Israelites and led them into freedom, into the Promised Land.[*]

So, Passover was an annual celebration of deliverance from the oppressor. Jesus and his disciples would have been among hundreds of thousands of people gathered in the city of Jerusalem to remember and celebrate this wonderful act. But it won't have escaped their notice that they were celebrating deliverance from the oppressor, but were very much

---

[*] Timothy Keller, *King's Cross: The Story of the World in the Life of Jesus* (pp. 161-162). Hodder & Stoughton. Kindle Edition.

oppressed. The oppressor was no longer Egypt, but Rome, but their state was very much the same. They sang songs of freedom and longed for that day when they'd be free. They longed for the arrival of the great liberator. Many of them had welcomed Jesus just days before. Perhaps he'd be the one to set them free.

This, then, is the context for these celebrations, and this most famous of meals. Jesus is about to join with his disciples to share in this celebration of Israel's redemption with this very special meal.

What strikes me at the beginning of the passage is the care with which this event, this meal has been planned. Look at verses 13-16. Two from his wider group of disciples – not among the original twelve – are sent into the city to meet a man carrying a jar of water (v.14) who will lead them to their venue, and they are given particular words to say to the owner of the house where they'll share in the Passover (v.15) – and the two will make the necessary preparations there. Jesus then joins them with the twelve disciples later (v.17). It seems very mysterious, very cloak and dagger, doesn't it? Has anyone ever planned a surprise birthday for someone? You have to go to extraordinary efforts to hide what you're planning. This is the sort of thing that's going on. But, why does Jesus seem to be taking such care? Why such secrecy?

Firstly – Jesus knows he is a marked man. We read just last week, after Jesus had cleansed the temple, in Mark 11:18, "The chief priests and the teachers of the law heard this and began looking for a way to kill him, for they feared him, because the whole crowd was amazed at his teaching." Jesus was popular with the crowds and the leaders suspect that he might be at the centre of a popular revolt against the Romans. They need to be rid of him. Because of his popularity they would need to find a way to arrest Jesus in secret, away from the crowds.

Second – Jesus knows there is a spy in his midst. Judas has already agreed to betray Jesus. This private meal with the disciples would give him the perfect opportunity to give away Jesus' location and allow the arrest to take place secretly. Jesus knows that Judas is the betrayer. This meal would be too important to be sabotaged, so Jesus has to keep the location of the meal from the twelve in order to keep it from Judas. This is why he arrives with the twelve later.

In fact, the first thing Mark records Jesus discussing with his disciples is this matter of his betrayal – that one of the companions gathered with him will betray him (v.18). The disciples are "saddened" by this and seek to reassure Jesus – and themselves, that they wouldn't do that. All Jesus will say, in verse 20, is that one of the twelve is responsible for the betrayal, and *"woe to that man who betrays the Son of Man! It would be better for him if he had not been born." (v.21)*

And it is with this rather sad note of death and betrayal, we move onto the meal itself. Of course, the ritual is so familiar – most weeks we repeat the remembrance of what's become known as the last supper more than once.

> *While they were eating, Jesus took bread, and when he had given thanks, he broke it and gave it to his disciples, saying, 'Take it; this is my body.'*
>
> *Then he took a cup, and when he had given thanks, he gave it to them, and they all drank from it.*
>
> *'This is my blood of the covenant, which is poured out for many,' he said to them.*
>
> (vv.22-24)

The meal that Jesus shares with his disciples is commonly assumed to be a Passover. But, if this is a Passover meal, isn't there something key missing? That's right, it's the lamb. Surely, if there were lamb at the table, instead of reaching for the bread, Jesus would reach for the lamb – he had also, after all, become known as the Lamb of God. No, this is not a

Passover meal. This is probably the meal that takes place on the day before Passover. But Jesus does make this a Passover meal with a twist – he takes the bread and wine and gives them a symbolic meaning that, if we're honest, we will probably never fully comprehend. He uses them to help his disciples – and all his disciples ever since – remember his death.

The two symbols of bread and wine were available pretty much throughout the Graeco Roman world – available to everybody, rich and poor. And this is precisely the point. Jesus gave us a feast that could be shared by everyone. Why? Because his love is for everyone. As we mentioned earlier, Jesus loved shared meals, didn't he – and he welcomed everyone to sit and eat with him. As Nick Page comments,

> Wherever he went, Jesus had meals with people, meals which satisfied not only their physical hunger and thirst, but also their spiritual hunger and thirst. The outsiders and the marginalised and the impure were welcomed around the table. This meal is the culmination of those traditions. And, indeed, this meal is to be shared with others; it's to be passed on, enjoyed and celebrated from day to day, week to week, generation to generation.[*]

This action of breaking bread and pouring out wine is also a prophetic act, like many other actions that week –

> With the body and the blood, the bread and the wine, we can see Jesus pointing ahead to his death. He knew, now, what was coming. He knew what fate awaited him. This is a meal that points ahead.

---

[*] Nick Page, *The Longest Week: The truth about Jesus' last days*, John Murray Press. Kindle Edition.

There is one other element to this moment of breaking bread – with his actions, Jesus is also telling a story. As Nick Page continues,

> We should not forget that this is Jesus' version of the Passover meal. And the point of Passover was to remember the story of Israel's rescue. The Passover meal … tells the tale through the elements. It celebrates the rescue of the Israel from slavery in Egypt. The unleavened bread symbolises the haste with which they have to leave; the sacrificial lamb is a reminder of the lamb that was slaughtered and its blood smeared on the doorposts for protection. Jesus clearly intended that his meal should tell the tale of his sacrifice. …
>
> In this upper room we have real bread, real wine: The ordinary stuff of life. transformed into the stuff of sharing and story and symbol.

And what does this all mean for us? Why is it so important? Because in the same way that when the Jews recounted – and still recount the story of that first great rescue, telling it as if the events took place yesterday, and not centuries, even millennia earlier, because they knew it was their story as much as the Israelites whose sons were spared because of the blood on the doorposts, this story is our story too. In Egypt that night, God's righteous judgment fell. Death visited every household, except the households of those who trusted in God for deliverance. They were spared because lambs were slaughtered and blood was daubed on their doorposts. Two thousand years ago, God's righteous judgement once again fell. Death should have visited, not just Israel, but the whole of humanity. Instead, one lamb was slaughtered that day. He was innocent. As we read in Isaiah, who prophesied about Jesus,

But he was pierced for our transgressions, he was crushed for our iniquities; the punishment that brought us peace was on him,   and by his wounds we are healed.
We all, like sheep, have gone astray, each of us has turned to our own way; and the Lord has laid on him the iniquity of us all.
(Isaiah 53:5-6)

He did this for us. He never did anything wrong. He was completely innocent of any wrongdoing, and he took the punishment, the sword of judgment that we deserved. My sin – my anger, lust, jealousy, judgmentalism, laziness – all of that was dealt with on the cross. He took the sword of judgment on himself that we might be set free. And he took that sword of judgement to give us new life. To give us fresh hope of the future. And that's where we'll leave this scene in the upper room with Jesus and the disciples. Taking the cup of wine, Jesus says, *"Truly I tell you, I will not drink again from the fruit of the vine until that day when I drink it new in the kingdom of God"* (v.25). One day he will drink new wine in the kingdom of God. Though death and pain will come, new life will spring up. The man who loved feasting so much, will hold a feast once more – and this time it'll last forever. This time, we will be invited. We will enjoy true feasting, true joy and gladness. There'll be no more pain or sadness. There'll be lots of laughter. Perhaps that's the reason we love to feast and eat together – it because when we are together in that way it is a foretaste of the day when, united with Jesus, with each other, and with all who have gone before us, we feast together in heaven forever. As Tim Keller summarises,

> Imagine you were in Egypt just after that first Passover. If you stopped Israelites in those days and said, "Who are you and what is happening here?" they would say, "I was a slave, under a sentence of death, but I took shelter under the blood of the lamb and escaped that bondage, and now God lives in our

midst and we are following him to the Promised Land." That is exactly what Christians say today. If you trust in Jesus's substitutionary sacrifice, the greatest longings of your heart will be satisfied on the day you sit down for that eternal feast in the promised kingdom of God.*

This story we've heard today is, as we're reminded in one of the Eucharistic prayers, our story. This is our story, this is our song.

Let's be full of gratitude to God, and let's make sure that the people around us don't miss out. Jesus gave himself for each and everyone who lives in our community. They need to know this. Who will tell them? Who will share the good news?

---

* Timothy Keller, *ibid* (p. 170)

The Victim and the Victory – Luke 22:63-23:25

Today we enter the incredibly murky world of Judean politics. It begins with brutality at the hands of the guards, who treat Jesus as their plaything. They mock him and beat him, blindfold him, demanding – "Prophesy, who hit you!" Why are they saying this? It's a sick joke; you see, their paymasters are Sadducees, who don't believe in prophecy. Ha ha ha.

Then the rulers leave him in some dingy prison cell while they work out what they will do with him, their prize. One thing's for certain, they are determined not to let this one get away; not after the things he's said or done. After all, let's not forget, he's made them look stupid in front of the crowd. To make matters worse, the crowd has lapped it up – he's become too popular for their liking. He's become a threat and Jerusalem isn't big enough for them and him.

So, as the night wears on and Jesus waits, they bring together a group who will pass judgement on him. The group is identified as the council of the elders of the people, both chief priests and temple of the law.

As Nick Page explains,

> The Sanhedrin was the supreme court of the Jewish nation. … It was … a tightly controlled council, convened at the request of the High Priest, serving at best as an advisory body and, at worst, as a bunch of yes-men. ..,. It consisted normally of seventy-one members, but only twenty-three were needed to pass a death sentence. It would have been perfectly possible for Caiaphas to convene twenty-two of his supporters.
> [Others who are there as the elders] probably means the city's elder statesmen. The picture is of a hastily convened meeting of the people with influence, the people who need to be kept

in the loop, so they can rubber stamp the decision that's been made.*

So, Jesus is led before this council, where they interrogate him. 'If you are the Messiah,' they said, 'tell us.'

Jesus replies, *'If I tell you, you will not believe me, and if I asked you, you would not answer."* (v.68)

In other word, Jesus says, whatever I say you will twist to suit your own agenda.

Jesus carries on, "from now on, the Son of Man will be seated at the right hand of the mighty God.'"

Nick Page writes,

It is the final statement of Jesus' destiny. He is the Messiah and he will usher in a new kingdom. It is not, we should note, Jesus' claim to be the Messiah that is blasphemous; the Jews did not view the Messiah as a divine figure. It is more likely the claim that he would one day be seated at 'the right hand of the mighty God' that meant, in their eyes, that Jesus was equating himself with God.

The interrogation continues, and the trap closes in. They've nearly got him … time to go for the kill.

'Are you then the Son of God?'

He replied, 'You say that I am.'

Then they said, 'Why do we need any more testimony? We have heard it from his own lips.'

(vv.70-71)

Nick Page asserts, "The decision to kill Jesus had been taken days, even months, ago. After his actions this week, whatever he said would have been taken as blasphemy." – and in their minds, this blasphemer has to die. The problem is, the ruling

---

* Nick Page, *The Longest Week: The truth about Jesus' last days*, John Murray Press. Kindle Edition.

council doesn't have the legal right to execute people – this had been removed from them by the Romans; and to maintain the appearance of legality, they need help, which is where Pilate comes in.

"Then the whole assembly rose and led him off to Pilate."
(Luke 23:1)

Pontus Pilate is Prefect of Judea. He's likely a military man, a career soldier, who has worked his way up the ladder until he was given command of Judaea. His role is to collect taxes for the Roman empire and to keep the population quiet. He'd have responsibility to ensure justice was administered, although he would only oversee the most important and high profile cases. As prefect he has the authority to deliver the death sentence to those criminals whose offences were deemed serious enough

At the time we encounter him, Pilate's position as Prefect is as insecure as a football manager whose team has gone on a losing streak. The man who appointed him had just been executed by the emperor, Tiberius. To try and placate Tiberius, Pilate dedicated a temple to him, but this didn't seem to win approval. Meanwhile, there was unrest under his rule in Judea, which he handled badly, leading to a letter of complaint being sent to Rome. This all threatens Pilate's increasingly tenuous grip on power, with riots and violence not far off. So, Pilate is walking a political tightrope: he is trying to please the emperor and placate the Jews. He needs the rulers on his side. He doesn't want any more trouble or difficult problems to deal with. But then, he comes face to face with Jesus.

The whole assembly leads Jesus to Pilate. It may not be far from the High Priest's house to Pilate's quarters in Herod's old palace. But it's far enough for the main charges against Jesus to have been altered completely.

What are their accusations? In short, a tissue of lies. *"We found this man perverting our nation, forbidding us to pay taxes to the emperor, and saying that he himself is the Messiah, a king."* (Luke 23.1–2) No blasphemy, then; no threat to the Temple; Pilate would hardly be swayed by that.

Instead, there is direct challenge to Roman rule. Jesus' accusers are framing the charges in the two terms that would be most likely to elicit a fierce response from the Romans: the refusal to pay taxes and the claim to be the real ruler. Flick back a chapter and see how they've twisted Jesus's words. Actually, he refused to answer their question about paying taxes; and he did say he was King, but of a completely different kingdom. But truth is there to be used as a tool – you can make people say what you want them to, as long as it suits you, can't you?

Evidently the man before Pilate doesn't look much like a king – as Nick Page comments,

> Pilate's question – 'Are you the King of the Jews?' – can hardly be serious. Jesus has been knocked about. He has been spat on and slapped. He has not slept for twenty-four hours. Pilate's sarcasm is met by Jesus' deadpan response: 'You say so.' So Pilate's immediate assessment of the situation is to dismiss the accusation (Luke 23.4). But the Temple authorities persist: 'He stirs up the people by teaching throughout all Judaea, from Galilee where he began even to this place' (Luke 23.6).

Pilate is clearly irritated – he doesn't want to have to deal with this problem. But then, he finds out that Jesus is from Galilee, so figures he can let the king of Galilee deal with it. Send the man to Antipas.

Herod Antipas is the same Herod who was responsible for the death of John the Baptist, as Nick Page explains.

> He is intrigued by Jesus. He's been eagerly anticipating the meeting; he had heard about Jesus and had wanted to see him

for some time (Luke 9.8). Perhaps he is hoping for debate and discussion, the kind of discussion he had enjoyed with John the Baptist. Perhaps he was merely hoping to be entertained, that Jesus would act like a court magician. Certainly he must have believed that he would be treated with the respect due his rank. None of these things happen. Jesus refuses to perform, refuses to debate, refuses even to speak. There's just a kind of embarrassing silence, which Antipas allows Jesus' accusers to fill with their vehement attacks. The interview ends in mockery and contempt. Powerless to make Jesus speak, Antipas exerts his power in a much more trivial way: by mocking Jesus and dressing him up like a doll (Luke 23.8–11)

When Jesus returns, Pilate takes one look at Jesus and says to the chief priests: *"I have examined him in your presence and have not found this man guilty of any of your charges against him. Neither has Herod, for he sent him back to us. Indeed, he has done nothing to deserve death."* (Luke 23:14-15).

Pilate hasn't taken long to make up his mind – Jesus is innocent. "I will have him punished and release him." Decision made. But this is where the crowd comes in. They shout, *"'Away with this man! Release Barabbas to us!' (Barabbas had been thrown into prison for an insurrection in the city, and for murder.)"* (vv.18-19)

Wanting to release Jesus, Pilate appeals to them again. But they keep shouting, *'Crucify him! Crucify him!'* (v.21)

For the third time he tries again: *"'Why? What crime has this man committed? I have found in him no grounds for the death penalty. Therefore, I will have him punished and then release him.'"* (vv. 22)

But with loud shouts they insistently demand that he be crucified, and their shouts prevail. *"So Pilate decided to grant their demand. He releases the man who had been thrown into prison for insurrection and murder, the one they asked for, and surrenders Jesus to their will."* (vv. 24-25)

Two questions I'd like to explore. Why did Pilate give into the crowd's demands and who exactly was the crowd anyway?

Firstly, let's look at Pilate. If he had wanted to release Jesus, he could have done. He could have held him in custody until after the festival. He could have ridden out the storm. But what good would that have done? He was a politician. The most pressing thing for him wasn't what's the right thing to do, but rather what would win him the most popular support. There is a choice between two political prisoners: Jesus, who apparently advocates non-payment of taxes and claims to be king, and Barabbas, a political revolutionary, a terrorist who has been involved in murderer. It's Pilate's version of an opinion poll: which execution is going to be more popular? He knows that the Temple aristocracy have handed Jesus over 'out of jealousy' (Mark 15.10). What he doesn't know is whether doing what the High Priest wants is going to cause him trouble. The answer is clear: in this crowd, Jesus has no popular support. This crowd want Barabbas.

So, who is the crowd? Not necessarily who we assume it to be. Almost ever since these events took place, it's been assumed that the Jews wanted Jesus dead; that the very same people who welcomed him into Jerusalem on Sunday, were now, only five days' later, baying for his blood. This idea is even conveyed in the Church of England liturgy, in one of the prayers we say in the Holy Communion service: "The crowds came out to see your Son, yet at the end they turned on him."[*] (The suggestion often follows that we too would do the same – welcome Jesus one day, and reject him the next.) But why? Why did the crowd change their minds so dramatically and turn against Jesus? Nick Page argues, "The answer is simple: they didn't."

---

[*] "Eucharistic Prayer D", *Common Worship: Common Worship: Services and Prayers for the Church of England,* Church House Publishing (2000) https://www.churchofengland.org/prayer-and-worship/worship-texts-and-resources/common-worship/holy-communion-service

It's perfectly clear from the Gospel accounts that the people were on Jesus' side, or, at least, enough of the people to make the Temple authorities unable to arrest him. Jesus' popularity was his shield. They were able to arrest him only in the early hours of the morning at an isolated place. Jesus had widespread popular support. … The idea that the entire Jewish population of Jerusalem somehow switched allegiance is just stupid.

So what was the nature of this crowd? There are two clues: the place and the time. The place is the courtyard of the prefect's HQ. It's unlikely that a large crowd of the general populace is going to be let in there. Also, this was all very early on the day of Preparation, a very busy day for the festival pilgrims. They had to get ready for the Passover festivities. The vast majority of pilgrims and citizens would be otherwise engaged at this time. So this is a carefully controlled mob. This is a crowd of supporters of the Jewish leaders – the gangs of the chief priests and leading families of Jerusalem. This is why the chief priests were able to stir up the crowd to do what they wanted (Mark 15.11): they were issuing instructions to their gangs. And the gangs decided that they would choose Barabbas.

There's been a lot to take in, hasn't there. How do you feel when considering all this? Angry? I feel that. Jesus is a political football. Innocent. He's done nothing wrong. What about shame? You see, although I don't believe the same people who were welcoming Jesus on Sunday then bayed for his blood, it does highlight the fickleness of human nature. I'm not saying we all would be the ones leading Jesus's beating, but if I were there, would I have courage to stop the brutality or would I join in, fearful of what others might think of me? Am I fearful of being seen to be weak?

Tom Wright reflects:

This doesn't only happen in guardrooms with soldiers. It also happens in offices and boardrooms, in school playgrounds and restaurant kitchens. It happens wherever people forget that every single other person they deal with is a beautiful, fragile reflection of the creator God, to be respected and cherished - and that they themselves are commanded, too, to reflect this God in the world. It happens, in other words, whenever people decide to make themselves feel good by making other people feel bad. Once again, we have all known what that's like.[*]

We may not have twisted the truth in order to have someone killed, but we have twisted truth for our own advantage, often at the cost of an innocent victim.

The events of that horrific night and early morning shine a light on the worst of our human nature.

Tom Wright continues,

I was once asked why Jesus died for the sins of the world … Luke is answering that question all through this passage. … the guards' bullying, the court's perversion of justice; all this and much more put Jesus on the cross. It wasn't just a theological transaction; it was real sin, real human folly and rebellion, the dehumanized humanity that has lost its way and spat in God's face. 'They said many other scandalous things to him'; yes, and we've all done so. As Luke leads our eyes to the foot of the cross he means us to feel not just sorrow and pity, but shame.

I'm going to close by sharing a reflection I wrote to imagine what it must have been like to be in the shoes of Barabbas, who, although he had plenty to be ashamed of, discovered the possibility of a second chance.

- - - -

---

[*] Tom Wright, *Luke for Everyone,* SPCK (2004)

Barabbas – A Second Chance

Right now, I should be dead, or dying, at least. I was involved in the uprising. The Romans call me a terrorist. I'd say I was more of a freedom fighter. The Romans deserve everything that's coming for them. Anyway, that's beside the point … the point is, I got caught and sentenced to death. I knew what that meant – the crosses are everywhere – a message to everyone that there's no messing with Rome, and soon I'd be on one. I was resigned to my fate. Nothing I could do about it.

But then, early in the morning, I was dragged out bound in front of the governor, Pilate, and the crowd. I heard something about a Jewish custom that meant a prisoner would be pardoned at Passover, and the crowd was given a choice – either I or another man, Jesus of Nazareth, could be freed. I looked over at this other man – first time I'd seen him. He certainly didn't look like your typical criminal. He was a political prisoner, apparently. Stitched up by the authorities, I reckon. Anyway, Pilate the Governor was trying to find out whose execution would be more popular – mine or his – so, here I was at the mercy of the crowd. "Who do you want me to release?" he asked, "Barabbas or Jesus who is called the Messiah?" Amazingly, the crowd cried out, "Barabbas" – my name. "And what do you want me to do with Jesus?" he asked once again. The crowd cried out, "Crucify him!" Pilate obviously smelt a rat, so he tried again. "But he's done nothing wrong." But the crowd got louder and angrier, crying out again, "Crucify him!" So Pilate washed his hands of Jesus – "his blood is on your hands," he said – and I found myself free.

I've been given my life back. Jesus took my place. There's no doubt in my mind that he's done nothing wrong, that he's an innocent man, and he took my place. I, the guilty one, have walked free. Life will be different from now on. It has to be different – I've been given a second chance. Better make the most of it.

Why Jesus did not save himself – Luke 22:26-56

We're now just two weeks before Easter, which is the most joyous day in the church's calendar, so it seems appropriate to be spending time this morning reflecting on the cross. There's no Easter without Good Friday, no resurrection without Jesus's death, no empty tomb without the cross.

Some of you will have a cross on a piece of jewellery, or perhaps tattooed somewhere. Others of you will have crosses in your house.

The cross is the logo of the Christian faith, which is kind of weird when you think that it was a form of execution. We don't go around wearing jewellery of electric chairs or gallows. And yet, we commemorate the most hideous form of execution ever invented. It's a bit ridiculous, isn't it? Well, the Romans certainly thought so. Christians were seen as weird and strange. Lies were spread about Christians, that they indulged in donkey worship. The message is clear – the Christians were fools.

After all, who on earth would worship someone who died like a criminal? It's just weird.

There's lots of mockery in our passage today …

The rulers sneer at Jesus, *"He saved others; let him save himself if he is God's Messiah, the Chosen One"* … (v.35)

The soldiers join in – they've seen the notice above Jesus's head *"This is the King of the Jews,"* and they can't resist the joke … *'If you are the king of the Jews, save yourself.'* (v.37)

Even one of the men on the cross can't resist joining in with the mockery –

One of the criminals who hung there hurled insults at him: 'Aren't you the Messiah? Save yourself and us!' (v.39)

I've read the account of Jesus's crucifixion a number of times and it still fills me with shock and horror. The problem is, I'm not sure I'd be so different to those men who treated Jesus so appallingly. We may see the worst of human nature here, but it's my human nature, not just those men back then. And this is why the cross really matters. This is why Jesus didn't do as the mockers suggested he should try and do – and come down off that cross and save himself.

Jesus stayed on that cross, submitted to death to deal with the hatred, selfishness and anger that messes up this beautiful world.

In the past couple of weeks as we've been coming to term with the Coronavirus that has changed our lives so dramatically and suddenly, we've seen the best of humanity – generosity, people reaching out to their neighbours, acts of kindness and love, the hard work and dedication of our NHS workers … the list could go on.

But we've seen the worst of humanity too … recklessness in ignoring advice not to gather in groups, selfishness in stockpiling, with people filling up their trolleys with toilet roll, and fighting in supermarkets, etc., but also the public shaming, anger and even hatred aimed at people who have done these things – this isn't right either.

Hang on a sec, we may say, I'm a good person – look at all the kind things I'm doing in this crisis. That's amazing – it's incredible that so many have volunteered to support the NHS in these times. I've been so proud of the way people in this church community have stepped up; however, sin is a problem for all of us. We need to understand the bad news….

There are four bad news stories of the Gospel.[*]

---

[*] This four point summary was taken a talk I heard given by Louie Giglio, author and pastor of Passion City Church.

1) No one is perfect. The only one perfect one is God almighty himself. Jesus was perfect, but he was God in human form. Every one else is imperfect. This is why the two words are etched behind the altar of Coventry's Old Cathedral – Father Forgive – not us, not them – but simply, Father Forgive – we are all complicit in the world's evil.

2) The consequences of not being perfect is that we have been separated from God. God being perfect can't have his perfection being compromised. Has anyone ever washed a white shirt with a brightly coloured sock? A sock is a small item isn't it, and yet it has disastrous consequences for the white shirt, which will never be the same.

3) Sin doesn't make us bad, sin makes us dead. Romans 6: 23, "the wages of sin is death. " The result of sin is death. Our sinful hearts leave us spiritually dormant and separated from God. The story isn't about how bad we are. None of us is good enough. Without Christ, sin leaves us dead. That's a problem.

4) No one can make themselves alive on their own. We didn't decide to be born. Had no choice in the matter. Had nothing to do with being alive. This was completely down to your mum and dad. In same way, as we're reminded by Romans 3:23 – "All of us have sinned and fallen short of the glory of God."

The result of our sin is spiritual death, and there is nothing we can do to get life.

So, that's the bad news. We need to get back to God, and yet he's so far beyond our reach. This is the bad news. Where does that leave us? Lost and hopeless.

But the story doesn't end there. God saw that there was no way we could reach him, nothing we could do to make ourselves right with him, so he took action. In Ephesians 2:4-5, *"because of his great love for us, God, who is rich in mercy, made us alive with Christ even when we were dead in transgressions – it is by grace you have been saved."* We were dead. Dead as a dodo. But God breathed new life into us.

Elsewhere Paul writes, *"God demonstrates his own love for us in this: While we were still sinners, Christ died for us"* (Romans 5:8).

God saw that there was nothing we could do to make ourselves right with him, and so he found a solution himself. Jesus is that solution. St. Paul writes in 2 Corinthians 5:21, *"God made him who had no sin to be sin for us, so that in him we might become the righteousness of God."*

Jesus became sin for us, took our sin away, destroyed it completely, so that we might be made completely pure. Completely. Because of Jesus and all he did for us, taking our sin away, we are completely acceptable to God. We can rest in his unchanging grace. We don't deserve it, which is why it's called grace.

This is why the day Jesus died is called Good Friday, as on that darkest of days Jesus lit up the world with the gift of forgiveness.

We see this happening in our reading – even as Jesus is being nailed to the cross, he cries out, *"Father, forgive them; they do not know what they are doing."* (Luke 23:34). What an extraordinary thing that Jesus is able to pray at that time.

Then we come to the extraordinary exchange between Jesus and the thief on the cross, which shows there is hope for each and every one of us.

- - - -

A Thief in Paradise

Wow, where am I? It's so beautiful here ...
Oh, hello, I didn't see you there. I can't take it in ... My name is
Judah, and I'm not a good man. No, I'm really not. I've done some
horrible things.
The thing is, I got caught. The Romans nabbed me, beat me and
sentenced me to be killed on one of those crosses.
Three of us were up on those crosses being crucified that day. One was a
criminal like me getting his just desserts, just like me. The other one
was different – a political prisoner. Claimed to be a King – and we all
know the only true king around here was the emperor. Anyway,
rumour has it that this guy, Jesus, had been very badly treated, that he
hadn't done anything wrong – just stitched up by the Jewish leaders.
Crucifixion is awful. The worst possible punishment. The beatings are
bad enough, but then they nail you to that cross. While we were being
nailed, me and this other robber bloke were swearing and cursing,
wishing we'd never been born. Jesus at first, didn't say a word, but then
he did. It was amazing. "Father, forgive them," he said, "They don't
know what they're doing." That's incredible. How can he say that?
He was innocent; it was a disgrace the way they'd treated him. Yet, he
could ask God to forgive them? They didn't deserve it, they deserved to
be punished, just like us. And yet he forgave them, just like he's
forgiven me. That's incredible.
Anyway, this man had to put up with awful insults being thrown at
him. They mocked him and spat at him. Again he said nothing, took
it all on the chin. Didn't get bitter or angry. Then the other guy started
joining in. "if you're who you say you are, why don't you save us and
yourself. As if you could."
I'd kept my mouth shut until then, but I couldn't stand it any more –
how could they do this to this bloke. He'd done nothing wrong! I turned
to the other thief and said, "don't you fear God? You should do! You
and I are guilty as sin. We've paid the price, we deserve to be here. But
this man has done nothing wrong! He's innocent. Just leave him
alone."

I don't know why I said the next bit, but something in him gave me hope – hope for someone like me. So, I turned to Jesus and said, "Jesus, remember me when you come into your kingdom." I knew he was a King, but not the usual sort of King. And I knew he was the only hope that I could possibly have. I wasn't expecting much; I didn't deserve much good to happen to me.

But he said something incredible; something I will never forget and always be thankful for. He turned to me and said, "today you'll be with me in paradise."

Me, a crook, a murderer, a scumbag, an awful, awful man, in paradise. I don't deserve it. I don't deserve to be loved in such a way. And yet, here I am. A thief in paradise. – and it's amazing. Why am I here? Because a crucified King opened the door and let me in. There is hope for people even like me – and it's amazing!

- - - -

Each of us needs to receive forgiveness from Jesus. He died for you and me. He went through that agony on the cross to restore our mean that our sin and brokenness is completely dealt with. The slate has been wiped clean. We are completely, fully forgiven.

There are two responses that flow from that – the first is gratitude. Saying thank you to God for the gift of forgiveness. Then, as forgiven people, we are called to forgive.

Actually, when people hurt us, forgiving them is rather hard to do. Some of us have experienced some terrible things and feel unable to forgive. Hard it sounds, we are called to forgive. I honestly believe God can give us the strength we need to do that. And actually, once we've done so, we find release for ourselves. Lewis Smedes said, "To forgive is to set a prisoner free and discover that the prisoner was you." On the flipside, bitterness and unforgiveness are poisonous. Unforgiveness ruins relationships within marriages, families, churches. Let's not be fooled. Forgiveness is costly and difficult, but unforgiveness is much more so.

Thanks to the cross of Jesus we are forgiven people. May we be full of gratitude. May we also, as forgiven people, be forgiving people. The world is in a mess, and the only solution is forgiveness – the gift God's given us, and the gift he calls us to give away. Only then can we bring healing to a hurting world.

The Power of the Cross – Mark 15:21-41 (sermon for Good Friday)

So much has been written about the cross – libraries full of books, fat and thin. Many wonderful songs, hymns and poems. So many different angles and perspectives have been taken. There is so much theology surrounding it – we hear of how Jesus died to save us from our sins, that he was the sacrificial lamb, the scapegoat who took the punishment that should have been meted out on us; we hear about how Jesus' death and resurrection signified his victory over the forces of evil and death. I could describe crucifixion and demonstrate that it really was the most barbaric method of killing ever conceived. I could spend time detailing how the extreme physical pain that Jesus went through on the cross was dwarfed by the spiritual pain of Jesus' separation from God, his Father.

All this stuff matters and it is important to read up on these subjects, because that way we can grow up and mature in our faith. But the question going round in my head as I have sought to prepare for this evening is simple. What message do we, the gathered church, need to hear today, on this particular Good Friday? What is the message of the cross for us?

I think there are two things that we need to hear and two things that we need to share with others.

The first is that the cross shows that **Jesus understands**. Whatever you're going through, there's a good chance that Jesus went through it too.

He knew what it was to be helpless – he couldn't carry his own cross and Simon of Cyrene was forced to carry it for him.

He knew what it was to suffer pain – the agony of the cross was unbearable, and that's not to mention the whipping and beating that he suffered beforehand.

He knew what it was to be insulted and persecuted. They had already got their way by having him sentenced him to death, but they weren't satisfied with that – their poisonous words rubbed salt into gaping wounds.

He also knew what it was to be publicly humiliated – they stripped him completely naked. There was no loin cloth to cover his modesty.

He knew what it was to be thirsty. Why is this significant? Because it's a helpful reminder that Jesus was completely human. Because we worship him as God, it is easy to forget this; but Jesus took on our humanity in all its frailty. It's also important, because if he hadn't been fully human, he wouldn't have been able to save us fully.

Finally, he knew what it was to be abandoned. Of his disciples, all fled apart from John and some of the women who watched on from a distance. Most of all, he knew what it was to feel like he'd been abandoned by God. God, his Father, to whom he'd always referred to as Father or Abba – Daddy. Instead, this time he cried out, "My God, my God, why have you forsaken me!" Jesus was crying out in protest against the experience of being abandoned. He had been forsaken by God and it broke him. This was the moment the Trinity seemed to be at breaking point in a way that simply defies understanding. It may seem like God was absent on the cross, but he wasn't. God wasn't absent at all – God the Son was on the cross, dying. God the Father suffered the grief of watching his beloved Son die in the most tragic way. God the Holy Spirit was there too, holding the whole Trinity together.

Through the cross, God experienced helplessness, persecution pain, humiliation, abandonment, and grief.

This means that when we experience those things, then God is standing right there with us. Whatever you're going through right now, God understands. You're not alone. When you weep, when you cry out in frustration or pain or loneliness, then God is crying out with you, because God knows what it's like to suffer.

So then, the first thing I want to share is that the cross shows that **Jesus understands**.

The second thing I want to share is that the cross shows that **Jesus loves you**. He went through all that stuff, all that awful stuff, the scourging, the mocking, the abandonment, the humiliation, the agony of the nails, for one reason and one reason only. Because he loves you. Because he loves me. I'll repeat that. Jesus died on the cross, because he loves you. Because that was the only way our broken relationship with God could be restored. Were you the only person on Earth, Jesus would still have died for you. Because he loves you that much, because you're worth that much.

You may not think you're very important or significant. That may be so in the eyes of the world. But the truth is that in God's eyes you are of infinite worth; not because of anything you've done; simply because you exist. God knit you together in your mother's womb. He breathed life into you. He made you in his image. He would do anything to maintain a relationship with you for the whole of eternity, including allowing himself to be abandoned, humiliated, persecuted, and crucified.

I remember reading the following on a bookmark when I was a teenager. It had such an impact that I turned it into a massive poster on my wall –

I asked the Lord how much he loved me. He said, "This much," stretched out his arms and died.

That's how much he loved me. That's how much he loved you.

The cross tells us that Jesus understands and that Jesus loves you. He gave everything for you.

So, how do we respond? Jesus gave everything. We need to

give everything back to him. As is expressed so beautifully in the famous hymn, "When I survey the wondrous cross",

Love so amazing, so divine,
Demands my soul, my life, my all!

The Beginning – Mark 15:37-16:7

When Jesus breathed his last, with a loud cry, everyone thought that it was the end of the story. The adventure was over. The man who had entered Jerusalem and had been welcomed as the promised king-Messiah by the crowds with such unbridled and almost raucous joy only 5 days previously was dead. The verdict was clear – he was yet another failed messiah – another man with grand ambitions who was either a conman who deliberately led others astray or was misguided – a madman who believed his own publicity and led many others along with him. His death at the hands of the Romans was proof that he wasn't who he was after all. Messiahs don't die. Well, real messiahs don't die. And everyone knew that Jesus had died. After all, the Romans were very good, experts, even, at many things – one of which was carrying out executions. They killed him alright – elsewhere, in John's Gospel, we learn that a centurion stabbed him with a spear to make sure he was dead, and blood and water came out to prove it. So, Jesus was dead, and his followers were left bereft.

In verses 40-41 we learn that some of his followers saw him die – some women, including *"Mary Magdalene, Mary the mother of James the younger and of Joseph, and Salome. In Galilee these women had followed him and cared for his needs. Many other women who had come up with him to Jerusalem were also there."*

The women had cared for him throughout his ministry, and in stark contrast to the disciples, who are nowhere to be seen, they stand by him to the very end. We don't know where the disciples are. Presumably they're in hiding, fearful that the same people who arrested Jesus would be after them. But the women stand by Jesus. They watch as Jesus' body is taken down, wrapped in cloths and laid in a tomb belonging to Joseph of Arimathea –a member of the Jewish council. This man has come out of the shadows and is prepared to risk his reputation by paying a final tribute to Jesus and putting his body to rest with the dignity it deserves. We are told in verse 47 that the women see where Jesus' body has been laid. Then, because it is the eve of the Sabbath, the day of rest, all goes deathly quiet.

So, it falls silent between Friday night and early Sunday morning. Jesus is dead, his body lying in a tomb secured by a huge boulder. His followers are in hiding, afraid for their lives. Meanwhile, the religious authorities are congratulating themselves on another job well done – another rebel got rid of – they've acted to save Jerusalem and the temple. They've ensured that they won't hear anything of Jesus and his followers again. If they had press spokesmen or newspapers, perhaps the reaction would have been something like this …

- - - -

One Saturday

A headline in the paper read
"Religious nut and freak is dead."

The spokesman for the Pharisees
Explained (while looking very pleased),
"This man had caused us lots of trouble,
We had to get him on the double.
He claimed he was the Chosen One,
Almighty God, His only Son.
We Pharisees weren't having that! –
Even worse, he claimed he'd sat
At God's right hand in heaven above
And will again. You know, I'd love
To see that day, but won't of course –
For that man's words are just a source
Of claptrap and of blasphemy,

That's why we killed him, can't you see?

He drew the crowds with clever tricks –
They even claimed he'd healed the sick.
The blind can see (or so they claim)
And crippled people walk again!
But that's not all – you'll laugh at this –
A dead man (said with emphasis)
Was brought back to life at his word –
This claim's preposterous, quite absurd.
We all know that dead men don't walk
About, or eat and drink and talk.
It's clear to me they've all been had.
Poor, simple people fooled – how sad!

At first we'd tried to humour him
Until he got beneath our skin.
He insulted us, called us snakes,
Told us that we were on the make.
We couldn't take it any more,
That really was the final straw.
We had him silenced, put to death,
This carpenter from Nazareth.
Let's see him speak against us now –
As he's dead, I can't see how!
He could rise again and death defy."
The spokesman spat, "And pigs might fly!"

- - - -

It's worth reiterating. No one expected Jesus to rise from the dead. He may have told the disciples more than once that he would die and rise again, but they didn't understand what he meant. It wasn't part of their plan – he wasn't meant to die. And now he had, the disciples would have been left in shock, numb with grief. Jesus had been everything to them. He had given them hope and, in the case of Mary Magdalene, he had brought her profound healing and acceptance, and new purpose, new hope. During his ministry they had been his faithful companions, looking after him and serving their Lord. Now, all of that had been dashed. The women stood by him, watching him die, because they had nowhere else to go, but by his side. And, when the day was dawning that Sunday morning, Mary Magdalene, Mary, the mother of James, and Salome, went to the tomb. Why? Because they wanted to serve him one last time, to express their love for him – in verse 16:1 we read that when the Sabbath had ended on the Saturday night, they *"bought spices so that they might go to anoint Jesus' body."* But when they get near the tomb, they realise there's a problem. We read in verse 3, *"they asked each other, "Who will roll the stone away from the entrance of the tomb?""* A large stone had been rolled across the entrance of the tomb on Friday evening and there was no way they could move it. What are they going to do? Are they going to be able to serve Jesus in the way they had hoped? And it is this that preoccupies them as they approach the tomb. They certainly aren't prepared for what they see when they get there …

> *But when they looked up, they saw that the stone, which was very large, had been rolled away. As they entered the tomb, they saw a young man dressed in a white robe sitting on the right side, and they were alarmed.*
> (vv.4-5)

The stone's been rolled away. They weren't expecting that. The message is clear here – they aren't expecting the tomb to be empty. They expected to greet and minister to Jesus' body. And their shock is increased by the presence of the young man sitting in the tomb.

What's happened? Where is Jesus?

"Don't be alarmed," he said. "You are looking for Jesus the Nazarene, who was crucified. He has risen! He is not here. See the place where they laid him. But go, tell his disciples and Peter, 'He is going ahead of you into Galilee. There you will see him, just as he told you.'"
(vv.6-7)

The young man tells them, that they are in the right place. Jesus was here – he'd been laid in the tomb, but he's not there any more. He has risen – they will meet him face to face once more. He, incredibly, has risen – just as he said he would be. And that's where the most reliable manuscripts of Mark's Gospel end, with the earth-shattering news that Jesus the Nazarene who had been crucified by the Romans is no longer in his tomb. He has risen. It's incredible, unbelievable even. And, as many people down the ages have said, this bit can't be true. Dead men don't rise. There must be another, more plausible explanation for the events that took place that day.

The tomb of Jesus is empty. This is the fact of history. It's worth spending some time looking at the possible explanations for this, because Mark anticipates them in his account …

1) **Jesus didn't really die**. Well, Mark says, actually, the centurion saw him die (15:39), and Pilate made sure that he was dead (15:44-45).

2) **The tomb was empty, but it was the wrong tomb** – actually, they saw where Jesus was buried (15:47). If it was the wrong tomb, wouldn't the authorities have pointed out the disciples' error once they went about proclaiming the good news. They would have gone to the correct tomb and pointed out where Jesus' body really was.

3) **The body was stolen** – but there was a large stone across the tomb (15:46), and in Matthew's account the tomb itself was guarded (Matthew 27:62-66).

4) **The disciples made up the resurrection.** We've seen already that they didn't believe Jesus when he told them he'd rise from the dead. If they believed it, why weren't they all there at the tomb waiting for Jesus to appear? Also, another telling detail was the fact that the only recorded witnesses in Mark's Gospel to this resurrection were women (16:1). I'm not being sexist, but I'm afraid that women didn't really count in Israel in Jesus' day. As Nick Page explains,

> Women were almost completely disqualified as witnesses in Jewish courts of law: the choice of women as the prime witnesses to the empty tomb would be a terrible piece of strategic planning, unless they genuinely were the first witnesses and the Gospel accounts were trying to get things right.[*]

Also, there's something else to consider – the disciples underwent a complete transformation – as Nick Page points out:

> Something changed these people into a force. Something turned a huddle of frightened peasants into a world-changing phenomenon. Personally, I have never been able to come up with an explanation for the growth of the early church and the persistence of belief in this man that didn't involve resurrection.

As Sherlock Holmes famously said, "Once you eliminate the impossible, whatever remains, no matter how improbable, must be the truth." Improbable as it seems, Jesus Christ really may have risen from the grave. He really might be alive. And if this is the case, you know what, everything changes. The

[*] Nick Page, *The Longest Week: The truth about Jesus' last days*

punishment for sin is death. We all have been given the death sentence for the sins we've committed. But when he died, Jesus the sinless one, took on our sin and took that punishment for us – as St Paul writes, *"God made him who had no sin to be sin for us, so that in him we might become the righteousness of God."* (Romans 6:23).

As Timothy Keller writes,

Jesus Christ came to pay the penalty for our sins. … he must have satisfied it fully, because on Easter Sunday he walked out free. The resurrection was God's way of stamping PAID IN FULL right across history so that nobody could miss it.[*]

Our sin – all of it – has been paid in full, and we can walk free. And, as Jesus says beautifully elsewhere in the Gospels, *"if the Son sets you free, you are free indeed"* (John 8:36).

That's the first implication – our sins are forgiven.

The second is that death doesn't have power any more. Because Jesus died and rose again, he defeated death – and if we have faith in him, we too will rise again. As Keller summarises,

In the Gospel of John, Jesus puts it this way:

"I am the resurrection and the life. He who believes in me will live, even though he dies; and whoever lives and believes in me will never die." (John 11:25–26)

His death means no death for us. His resurrection means our resurrection.

"We believe that Jesus died and rose again and so we believe that God will

---

[*] Timothy Keller, *King's Cross: Understanding the Life and Death of the Son of God* (p. 137). John Murray Press. Kindle Edition.

bring with Jesus those who have fallen asleep in him."
(1 Thessalonians 4:14)

This is incredible. We have hope, because of Jesus. We can look death in the face, because Jesus has removed its sting. He has won the victory. There is hope for tomorrow.

There is also hope for today. ... Because Jesus is risen, we know our future is secure in him. This means that we can face whatever happens to us in that light.

If I face sickness or death – I know my hope is secure in Jesus.

If I face money troubles – I know my hope is secure in Jesus.

If I face the grief of losing loved ones - I know my hope is secure in Jesus.

I don't need to rely on money or reputation to secure my identity. Why? Because my hope is secure in Jesus.

People may threaten to hurt and harm me, but I'm going to be ok, because I know my hope is secure in Jesus.

I may experience suffering and hardship – I know my hope is secure in Jesus.

I can take risks because I know my hope is secure in Jesus.

I can be free from ultimate anxiety, because I know my hope is secure in Jesus.

Because Jesus is alive, this broken and hurting world will be redeemed and be made even more glorious than it is now. I want to close by reading this wonderful summary of the hope we have because of the resurrection:

The resurrection means we can look forward with hope to the day our suffering will be gone. But it even means that we can look forward with hope to the day our suffering will be glorious. When Jesus shows the disciples his hands and his feet, he is showing them his scars. The last time the disciples saw Jesus, they thought those scars were ruining their lives. ... Seeing Jesus Christ with his scars reminds them of what he did for them—that the scars they thought had ruined their lives actually saved their lives. Remembering those scars will help many of them endure their own crucifixions.

On the Day of the Lord—the day that God makes everything right, the day that everything sad comes untrue—on that day the same thing will happen to your own hurts and sadness. You will find that the worst things that have ever happened to you will in the end only enhance your eternal delight. On that day, all of it will be turned inside out and you will know joy beyond the walls of the world. The joy of your glory will be that much greater for every scar you bear.

So live in the light of the resurrection and renewal of this world, and of yourself, in a glorious, never-ending, joyful dance of grace.*

---

* Keller, *King's Cross* (p. 140).

The Breath of New Life – Mathew 28:1-10 (Easter Sunday Sunrise Sermon 2014)

This morning, we're going to journey together to Narnia.

The land of Narnia was under the spell of the White Witch: it would always be winter; spring would never come. All who lived in Narnia lived in fear of the witch's power. She could use her evil powers to turn people into lifeless statues. Their only hope was in the coming of the great lion, Aslan, who, they hoped, would come and restore all things. Lucy, Edmund, Susan, and Peter entered Narnia through the back of a wardrobe. The coming of these Sons of Adam and Daughters of Eve was a bad omen for the White Witch. She managed to tempt young Edmund into betraying his brother and sisters and ultimately Aslan himself. …

When the White Witch finally confronts Aslan face-to-face she demands that Edmund be given to her:

> "You know that every traitor belongs to me as my lawful prey and that for every treachery I have a right to a kill. … that human creature is mine. His life is forfeit to me. His blood is my property."[*]

Aslan speaks to the witch alone and then sadly tells the children that the matter has been settled. Unknown to the children, Aslan has agreed to give his own life in the place of Edmund. That night, Lucy and Susan follow Aslan to the Stone Table. They watch the horrible proceedings as Aslan allows himself to be placed on the table, tied with ropes, and have his mighty mane shaved off. The girls watch as the ogres and hags hit him and spit on him. The White Witch takes up a

---

[*] C.S. Lewis, *The Lion, the Witch and the Wardrobe (The Chronicles of Narnia)*, HarperCollins Children's Books

knife and prepares for the execution. Bending down she speaks to Aslan for the last time,

> "And now, who has won? Fool, did you think that by all this you would save the human traitor? Now I will kill you instead of him as our pact was, and so the Deep Magic will be appeased. But when you are dead what will prevent me from killing him as well? And who will take him out of my hand then? Understand that you have given me Narnia forever, you have lost your own life, and you have not saved his. In that knowledge, despair and die."

That night Susan and Lucy "cried till they could cry no more. … the sadness and shame and horror of Aslan's death … filled their minds."

Although Narnia is a fantasy world, it isn't that far from our world. Always winter, never Christmas. This is like the effect of evil in our world. It affects everybody in some way or another. The world is not the place it should be. There are places where people are fighting and killing each other. There are places where many are sick. There are places where people die because they don't have enough food Closer to home, if we're honest, our families, our schools, our church – they're not perfect either. Like the people of Narnia, we are under the spell of evil, and there's nothing we can do to defeat evil. We cannot make the spring come. We need a rescuer.

This was how the world found itself on Good Friday. We were in a mess and had no ability to fix things. We needed a Saviour. Jesus was that Saviour. Though he'd done nothing wrong, he gave up his life in our place. And on Good Friday, when Jesus died, the world seemed in even more of a mess, because an innocent man died. Jesus' friends were devastated.

Meanwhile, in Narnia … Susan and Lucy saw Aslan die. They stayed by his body and wept. But then …

At that moment they heard from behind them a loud noise—a great cracking, deafening noise as if a giant had broken a giant's plate.... The Stone Table was broken into two pieces by a great crack that ran down it from end to end; and there was no Aslan. … They looked round. There, shining in the sunrise, larger than they had seen him before, shaking his mane (for it had apparently grown again) stood Aslan himself.

Aslan has come back to life. By offering himself in the place of Edmund, he has broken the curse – in his words, death itself has rolled back. The everlasting winter comes to an end – spring comes. Aslan defeats the Witch, and then he breathes new life into the statues. All is restored and made new once more.

When C.S. Lewis wrote *The Lion, the Witch and the Wardrobe*, he clearly meant for us to see parallels between Aslan and Jesus, between the moment Aslan willingly lays down his life to save Edmund the betrayer, and the way that Jesus willingly went to the cross. Jesus had done nothing wrong. He was innocent, and he took our place. When Good Friday was over, it seemed like a tragedy. It was the saddest day. Like Lucy and Susan in *The Lion, the Witch and the Wardrobe,* Jesus' friends had watched him die. They were so sad. There would have been many tears. They wanted to go to the tomb to be close to him somehow, so they went as soon as they could, early on Sunday morning. But Jesus' body wasn't in the tomb. They met an angel, who told them something amazing …

> *"Do not be afraid, for I know that you are looking for Jesus, who was crucified. He is not here; he has risen, just as he said. Come and see the place where he lay"*
> (Matthew 28:5-6)

They looked, and incredibly, the angel was right – the tomb was empty. Jesus had gone. But then, something even more amazing happened …

So the women hurried away from the tomb, afraid yet filled with joy, and ran to tell his disciples. Suddenly Jesus met them. 'Greetings,' he said. They came to him, clasped his feet and worshipped him. Then Jesus said to them, 'Do not be afraid. Go and tell my brothers to go to Galilee; there they will see me.'
(vv.8-10)

They met Jesus himself face to face. Imagine the joy they must have felt! It changed everything. Suddenly, what looked like the greatest defeat was actually the greatest victory. In dying, Jesus took on all of our sin, he stepped in our place. He took on death itself. By rising again, Jesus broke the curse of sin. Death itself has been defeated. This is the story of easter. This is what we've gathered today to celebrate.

Without Jesus all we would have to look forward to would be an everlasting winter of sadness, sickness and an eternity of darkness. The world is blighted by the dark magic of evil that brings death and suffering. But Jesus came so we could experience spring. He came to bring new hope and breathe new life to the world. At Easter, a deeper magic brought Jesus back to life and now Jesus Christ brings life to the whole world. He saves us when we've messed up and he brings life and meaning to every day.

Sometimes we act as if we're frozen, and we think that God isn't powerful enough to bring summer in our lives. Maybe our problems are too big. The empty tomb tells us that there is no problem that is too big for Jesus to help us with. The tomb is empty. He is alive. There's a wonderful moment in the Gospels after he's risen again, when Jesus breathes on the disciples, and says to them, receive the Holy Spirit. He breathes life into them and it brings about huge transformation for them. We're here today, because of that transformation, because they went from being in hiding, to fearlessly proclaiming that Jesus is risen. Jesus says to us too, I can bring that transformation in your life, if you'll let me. Will we do that, will we let Jesus breathe new life into us?

Some of us might see the Easter story as just a nice story, like Narnia. But what if it's more than that? What if the tomb is really empty? What if he really has taken away our sin and given us new life?

In the Bible, A man named Nicodemus went to Jesus and asked him how to get to heaven. Nicodemus was probably a better person than any of us. He was a leader of Israel, a man who studied the scriptures, quoted the scriptures, sang the scriptures. He obeyed all the laws of God. You would expect Jesus to pat him on the back and say "Well done. Heaven is waiting for you." But he doesn't. Jesus says, "You must be born again." And that means to give God all of your heart and all of your life. Some of us might want to do that today. If you would like to, then please join with me in praying the following prayer …

> Dear Lord Jesus,
> Thank you that you died on the cross in my place so that I could be forgiven.
> Thank you that you rose again to bring new life and new hope to the world.
> Would you come in my heart and breathe new life in me.
> Help me to follow you every day of my life.
> Amen.

Rising from the Rubble – Ezekiel 37:1-14 and Mark 16:1-8 (Easter Sunday Sunrise Sermon 2015)

In the year 2000 Dresden's Frauenkirche (Church of Our Lady), its most iconic church, was still a pile of rubble. While other buildings around it were being rebuilt and the city was being gradually being restored some of its former glory, the building that had once been the jewel in Dresden's crown, remained desolate, a stark reminder of the destruction that swept through the city on two fateful nights in February 1945. Until that day it had had a glorious history and people thought it'd last forever, but then the bombs poured down on the city and two days later the building collapsed. It was a stark reminder of the ruin you can face if you lose your way. And it did lose its way. In 1938, the Pastor Hugo Hahn was expelled, because he had faced up to Hitler and the blight of Nazism. From then on, false doctrine, hatred and racism was preached from the pulpit of the Frauenkirche. As the Jewish synagogue burned down in November 1938 and Jews were increasingly persecuted, no action was taken – everyone passed by on the other side. That night a vagrant prophesied that the fire would return to the city. And indeed, in 1945 the fire rained down and destroyed the city. Two days later, the church itself crumbled. The city and its jewel, the church lay in ruins, and hope was gone. The dream had died.

They thought they were invincible, the chosen ones. They thought they would stay in the Promised Land forever. They ignored the warnings of the prophets who told them they'd only stay in the land if they obeyed God. They didn't really think God would allow that to happen to his people. But it did. In 597BC, the Babylonians came. Judah and Jerusalem, God's own city, were no more. The king and many others with him were taken into exile. The city and its jewel, the temple lay in ruins, the people had been exiled, no longer in their promised land, no longer chosen, but surely, forsaken. Hope was gone. The dream had died.

What a wonderful few years it had been! The disciples went from nobodies to followers and friends of the most extraordinary man who ever lived, the man they knew was God's anointed king – no one else could teach so incredibly or do such works of power. Then, he entered Jerusalem and was welcomed as the true king. This would be the time when he would sweep to glory, kicking out the Romans, and they would rule the kingdom with him. They didn't really listen or understand when he'd told them he'd be captured, tried and killed by the chief priests, but he didn't really mean it, did he? And then, as they shared that wonderful intimate meal with him, he told them he was going to die. He wouldn't really, would he? But he did. When the soldiers came, when one of their own betrayed him, they all fled, leaving their leader alone. Most of them were still in hiding when they heard the news he'd been crucified. Now, with his death, hope was gone. The dream had died.

I wonder if you feel like the people from Dresden, or the nation of Israel, or indeed the disciples. You feel like your life's been ruined and that hopes have been dashed. Perhaps it's been due to bereavement, or ill-health, or unemployment. Perhaps life hasn't worked out in another way in the way you'd hoped. Perhaps we feel like that about work, church, family, marriage, self, etc. Perhaps we feel dry.

Either way, this sense of disappointment hangs like a cloud over you, and you can't shake it off. The dream has died.

The dream had died. They were in exile. They'd lost their land, their identity, their temple. They felt forsaken and ashamed, like dry bones. Filled with despair and hopelessness. But then God gave Ezekiel a vision of a valley of dry bones.

He commanded Ezekiel to speak to the bones, and tell them that they'll come to life. Ezekiel did so. The bones became corpses. When he spoke again, breath filled the corpses, and they came to life. A vast army. Dry bones no more. Where death reigned, new life had sprung up. The impossible had happened. Hope was restored. And then the word of the Lord came to Ezekiel once more …

'Son of man, these bones are the people of Israel. They say, "Our bones are dried up and our hope is gone; we are cut off." Therefore prophesy and say to them: "This is what the Sovereign Lord says: my people, I am going to open your graves and bring you up from them; I will bring you back to the land of Israel. Then you, my people, will know that I am the Lord, when I open your graves and bring you up from them. I will put my Spirit in you and you will live, and I will settle you in your own land. Then you will know that I the Lord have spoken, and I have done it, declares the Lord."'
(Ezekiel 37:11-14)

Though desolate and hopeless now, hope would be restored once more. The exiles would return. Seventy years later they were freed from their captivity and returned home.

Six hundred years later, clouded by grief, the women went to Jesus' tomb to anoint his body for burial, but something happened that changed everything for them, something that they didn't expect.

But when they looked up, they saw that the stone, which was very large, had been rolled away. As they entered the tomb, they saw a young man dressed in a white robe sitting on the right side, and they were alarmed.
(Mark 16:4-5)

To add insult to injury, someone had obviously tampered with Jesus' grave and removed his body. No wonder they were alarmed. What on earth was this figure in white doing, and what had he done with Jesus? If the presence of the man was extraordinary, then his words were even more so …

> *'Don't be alarmed,' he said. 'You are looking for Jesus the Nazarene, who was crucified. He has risen! He is not here. See the place where they laid him. But go, tell his disciples and Peter, "He is going ahead of you into Galilee. There you will see him, just as he told you."' (vv.6-7)*

Jesus was here – he was crucified, they were in the right place. His body had lain in this tomb. But He has risen – he was alive, and he will meet with them again. And this bit is important … *Just as he told you.*

You see, Jesus had told them that this would happen. In Mark 8:31, we read, *"the Son of Man must suffer many things and be rejected by the elders, the chief priests and the teachers of the law, and that he must be killed and after three days rise again."*

Despite this, none of the disciples really believed Jesus would die. They didn't understand this was part of God's plan for saving the world. Then when Jesus was dead, they thought it was all over. No one was expecting to see Jesus again. It had seemingly all gone terribly, terribly wrong. So, no wonder the women are full of shock and fear. No wonder the other disciples are nowhere to be seen. It would only be later when the fearful disciples met with their saviour face to face that the fear would be replaced by peace, and when they would be given fresh life and purpose, when new life would be breathed into their dry bones.

And Jesus' resurrection brings hope to us. Although we may feel that our dream has died, that we are like the dry bones, the word of the Lord comes to us. At times like these, we especially need to heed God's command to Ezekiel and his people. "Hear the word of the Lord" – In tough times, we need to cling to God and believe his promises. The Bible contains the words of eternal life. It contains the living words of the resurrected Lord Jesus who died for you and me. Believe God's Word. Cling to his promises. You may see your circumstances and say that nothing can overcome them, but God is bigger. His word stands. Life works best when we fix our hope on the Rock of God's Word. The Word that tells us,

"With God, all things are possible." (Matthew 19:26)

"I will never leave you or forsake you." (Deuteronomy 31:8)

The Word that speaks to us and says, *"Dry bones,"* though you may be desolate and dry, though you may feel in pieces, and you want to give up, hear this promise, *"I will put breath in you, and you will come to life. Then you will know that I am the Lord.'"* (Ezekiel 37:6)

Hear the word of the Lord. God will breathe new life into you. He specialises in bringing hope out of hopelessness and fresh purpose to those who feel they've lost their way. Indeed, I believe that often what comes after our place of brokenness is greater than what came before. I believe this is the case, whether we've been through a challenging time, whether we've been rocked by hardship or bereavement, God is at work, he is shaping us into an army ready to fight for him, that he is calling us to put our trust in him. The wind of the spirit is at work among us, bringing new life to dry bones.

The same spirit, the same breath of life speaks to you, and says, come back to life. I will restore you. I can give you fresh hope. We know that God will keep his word to us, because the tomb is empty. Jesus is alive. In the words of the worship song, "Death, where is your sting? Our resurrected King has rendered you defeated."*

---

* "Forever", performed by Bethel Music and written by Brian Johnson, Kari Jobe, Jenn Johnson, Gabriel Wilson, Joel Taylor, Christa Black Gifford

Ten years ago, the Frauenkirche opened its doors and a new ministry began. The building had been fully restored with a mixture of old and new stones. Of course, it's more than a building. The worshipping community has been given fresh purpose and a fresh vision for the future. They're stepping out into their calling to be a people of peace, reconciliation and forgiveness. As a visible reminder of this calling, there is a Coventry Cross of Nails at the heart of the church on their altar. They haven't forgotten their past brokenness, but out of that past has come a new beginning. God has made something new. He's using their brokenness for his greater glory. It's a wonderful testimony to the way God can bring beauty out of brokenness. He did that for the disciples, and he can do that for each of us. God can give us each fresh vision and purpose. He can give us strength to begin again. He has immeasurably more for us than we can ask or imagine.

> *"I will put my Spirit in you and you will live, … Then you will know that I the Lord have spoken, and I have done it,' declares the Lord."*
> (Ezekiel 37:14)

The Resurrection Changes Everything – 1 Corinthians 15:1-8; 19-26, 55-58, Matthew 28:1-10 (Easter Sunday 2017)

How do you view the Easter story as we've heard it this morning? The danger is that we become so familiar with the story that it becomes like a fairy story shrouded in the mist of time, describing events that happened so long ago that we can't see their relevance for us. I'd like to invite us to take a fresh look. Notice the grief and confusion that pervades the atmosphere. Notice how the women, identified as Mary Magdalene, Joanna, Mary the mother of James (v.10) are struck with bewilderment when they find that Jesus' body has apparently been moved from the tomb, and then utter terror when two men appear out of nowhere to tell them that Jesus isn't in the tomb, because he's been raised from the dead. Notice the disbelief that fills the room when the disciples hear the women recounting the encounter at the empty tomb. They have no doubt that the women's words are "nonsense" (v.11). Notice how Peter, the leader of the disciples is still left wondering what's happened (v.12) when he goes to the tomb and finds it empty with only the grave clothes in place. Why does this all matter? I want to suggest that if this were all a nice fairy tale that the disciples had made up, they would have made themselves look better, like they expected Jesus to rise again all along – after all, he had told them enough times that this would happen, hadn't he? But this, of course, isn't how the events unfold in the Bible. Instead it's clear that what had happened between Maundy Thursday and Easter Sunday was viewed by the disciples as nothing less than an utter disaster.

We need to notice the atmosphere of confusion and fear that pervades that Easter morning. This matters, because the people who deserted Jesus when he was arrested and crucified and who went into hiding after his death, fearful for their own lives were the very same people who weeks later proclaimed boldly that Jesus was alive. They were the same people who ended up giving up everything for this claim, including their lives.

One has to question, what's behind this transformation, because something has to explain it. No one really disputes that Jesus body had gone from the tomb that Sunday morning. What they dispute is why. People claim the disciples simply made up this story, but if this is the case, you have to ask yourself, why would they then be willing to suffer persecution and many of them to die for what they knew to be a lie? It's impossible that this would be the case. So we're left with the extraordinary possibility that Jesus really did rise from the dead and that they were transformed through their encounter with the risen Jesus. Nothing else adequately explains the transformation we witness in the disciples, whose belief in the risen Jesus went on to change the world. As Sherlock Holmes famously said, "when you have eliminated the impossible, whatever remains, however improbable, must be the truth."

If it is the truth that Jesus rose from the dead, this has world changing implications – and implications for me and you today. I'd like to examine them for a while, and in particular the words the men spoke to the women at the tomb:

He is not here; he has risen! Remember how he told you, while he was still with you in Galilee: 'The Son of Man must be delivered over to the hands of sinners, be crucified and on the third day be raised again.' "
(Matthew 28:6-7)

The men are clear – although the events of Holy Week and Easter didn't happen according to the plan of the disciples, as far as Jesus was concerned, it always had to happen this way.

"The Son of Man must be delivered over to the hands of sinners, be crucified and on the third day be raised again."

Why is this? Why did it need to happen this way?

In one of his letters Paul has a go at trying to articulate what you'd be left with if you were to strip everything else away and be left with the heart of the good news of the Christian faith. He writes ...

> *[This is] of first importance: that Christ died for our sins according to the Scriptures, that he was buried, that he was raised on the third day according to the Scriptures,"*
> (1 Corinthians 15:1-3)

That's it – simple. Everything else is detail. So, answering the question I posed a moment ago – why was it that Jesus had to die? He had to die "for our sins".

We might raise our eyebrows and suggest that sin's an outdated concept, but we only need to look at the cause of most of the suffering that happens in this world, and it's safe to say that sin responsible for most of it. When God created humanity, he gave us free will. Why? So we could choose to love. So we could choose to love him and each other. Love is not love unless it's chosen. God gave us the choice, and we chose to go our own way. We rejected him and crowned him as king of our own lives. As the prophet Isaiah lamented, *"We all, like sheep, have gone astray, each of us has turned to our own way;"* (Isaiah 53:8).

It's not a popular thing to say nowadays, because we're all convinced that we're good people, but the reality is that we're sinners – every one of us.

Sin is a virus and it's killing this world, and it's infected all of us – and we can't do anything about it. Each and every one of us needs a Saviour. Every one with out exception.

God saw this – he saw the mess we make of our lives, and of our world. God saw that we couldn't save ourselves, and so he became our Saviour. In the words of John 3:16–17

"For God so loved the world that he gave his one and only Son, that whoever believes in him shall not perish but have eternal life. For God did not send his Son into the world to condemn the world, but to save the world through him."

Because of Jesus we can know forgiveness and freedom from the bad things that we've done, and from the burdens of hurt that we carry. Jesus took all our sin and brokenness on himself on the cross. As St Paul writes elsewhere, *"God made him who had no sin to be sin for us, so that in him we might become the righteousness of God."* (2 Corinthians 5:21). Thanks to Jesus the slate has been wiped clean. This is why Good Friday is such an important day in the life of the church, because we remember. We remember that his death was not simply an accident or a miscarriage of justice. It wasn't about one man's attempt to fight the tyranny of Rome and the hypocrisy of those who ran the temple. No, Jesus had his sights much higher than that. Jesus was fighting a much bigger battle. He had bigger fish to fry. On the cross Jesus took on two deadly enemies – sin and death – and he won. By rising again, Jesus defeated death. No matter what happens, we can know true hope that looks death in the face, because we too will rise again. Death has lost its power over us.

I don't know where you're at in your faith at the moment, where you place yourself in the Easter story. Are you like the disciples, who have heard about these events, but you're bewildered by them? I believe we can all meet with the risen Jesus and I believe that such an encounter with him could change our lives.

We need to do 2 things in response to the Good News of the Gospel –

1. No matter how rich, poor, sophisticated we are we are called to repent of our sin. Before we repent, we face death. But we are called to turn and face Jesus Christ, the One who is Life. We will know in our hearts of hearts whether we're facing Christ or not. God has an offer - my Son died on that cross for you to take away your sin. He waits for you with open arms. Will you turn round and say, "Jesus I want to follow you – I believe you died on the cross for me. Will you forgive me?"

2. Live for Jesus Christ - full on. Not a soft option – this will totally cost you. The road of obedience is a narrow one. It's hard to follow Jesus. If we decide that we want to follow him, it will impact time, commitment, wallet, everything. *

This may seem like a tough ask, but Jesus can give us true peace. He will make us the person we want to be – and more – and will use us to do some fantastic things. He has amazing plans and purposes for us as a church and as individuals. We can know the unsurpassable glory of God in our lives. We can know true peace.

We have a destiny in front of us, but we must choose. Decide to live for Jesus and obey him. Tough call.

Jesus Christ died for you and me so that we could become resurrection people. Could be knocked down in life, but not knocked out. On the floor. Jesus can lift you up. Rose from the dead to show the curse of death is defeated. All the obstacles and obstructions can be dealt with and we can know peace. Can become resurrection person right now.

---

* This is a summary of the challenge given by Carl Beech at the CVM Gathering conferences.

I'd like to invite you to make response this morning.

Some of us have never made a commitment to God. Now might be the time to make that first step of faith.

Others of you used to believe, perhaps when you were children, but you've drifted away. God wants you to come back home. He wants to pour his love into your lives.

Some of you know who Jesus is, but you're sitting on the fence – this is a painful place. It's time to make a decision. Choose who you will serve - yourself or the living God.

Now's an opportunity to come home, to join the family of the kingdom of God, to become the people we've been made to be – resurrection people.

> There's a verse in the Bible that says
> *"For I am not ashamed of the gospel, because it is the power of God that brings salvation to everyone who believes"*
> (Romans 1:16)

Actually, some of us know we have acted as if we're ashamed of the Gospel, when God is calling us to speak out that Jesus is alive, and we've kept quiet. Perhaps we would like to declare today that we will be open about our faith and proclaim to friends, neighbours and family that Jesus is alive. We live in an increasingly desperate world full of fear and hopelessness. Jesus is the only hope, the only certainty in this world, and we are his messengers, called to proclaim his gospel. As Archbishop Justin said recently, "For he is completely true, completely faithful, completely trustworthy. He simply asks us, his servants, to live in a way that witnesses to him in this world."[*]

---

[*] "'The only certainty in the world is Jesus Christ' - Archbishop speaks at New Wine conference",

If you'd like to respond to any of these, whether you want to commit yourself to Christ for the first time, or whether you'd like to come back home, or whether you'd like to be someone who is no longer ashamed of the Gospel, then I'd like to invite you to stand where you are, and we can pray for each other. I know you won't regret it. Let today be your resurrection day, because Christ is risen. He is risen indeed, Alleluia.

Dear Lord Jesus,
Thank you that you died on the cross in my place so that I could be forgiven.
Thank you that you rose again to bring new life and new hope to the world.
Would you come in my heart and breathe new life in me.
Help me to follow you every day of my life.
Amen.

https://www.archbishopofcanterbury.org/speaking-and-writing/speeches/only-certainty-world-jesus-christ-archbishop-speaks-new-wine

Breaker of Chains – Mark 16:1-8 (Easter Sunday Sunrise Sermon 2018)

He was born in obscurity in a far flung part of the Roman empire. His people languished under the brutal hand of a military dictatorship, who enforced Roman rule through fear. If we want to know what it must have felt like to be the Israelites living in such conditions, we could think of Syria and Iraq a couple of years ago when ISIS took power, or huge parts of Europe that suffered under the Nazi occupying forces seventy five or so years ago.

The Emperor Nero was said to have declared,

> I am the arbiter of life and death for the nations: it rests in my power what each man's lot and death shall be: by my lips Fortune proclaims what gift she would bestow on each human being: from my utterance peoples and cities gather reasons for rejoicing; without my favour and grace no part of the whole world can prosper; all those many thousands of swords which my peace restrains will be drawn at my nod…[*]

Fear reigned in Israel two thousand years ago. The Israelites were very much a forgotten people. Oppressed, defeated. They were prisoners in their own Promised Land. Even though the symbol of the temple was one of the wonders of the ancient world, beneath the surface all was not well. After all, it was all very well having this magnificent building, which became the ultimate place of pilgrimage for Jews throughout the Roman Empire, for the poorer residents of Jerusalem, which were the vast majority, their main concern was survival. When you are near starving, when there's no work for you, when you have little more than the clothes on your back, what joy can you take in the marble-clad Temple on the hill? After

---

[*] As cited in Klaus Wengst, *Pax Romana and the Peace of Jesus Christ* (Philadelphia: Fortress, 1987), 47.

all, most people were excluded, unable to attain the levels of purity needed to access the most sacred parts of the Temple Mount. Unable to pay for the sacrifices that their religion required.

As for the temple elite, they were hated almost as much as the Romans, for they colluded with them – they had to, or they would have lost their tenuous grip on power.

This, then, was the society into which Jesus was born, and within which he worked, taught and performed his miracles: a Roman province, governed at the local level by an illegitimate leadership under the rule of a pagan empire; a military dictatorship which saw its subjects as a means of producing wealth; a place where there was a huge gulf between rich and poor and where, for the bulk of people, a life of grinding poverty was made worse by the knowledge that there were 'soldiers' boots just above their head'. No wonder so many people were looking for a rescuer, a hero, a Messiah.

They looked for the one who would rescue and liberate them, bring them freedom – freedom from the Romans. They imagined a great leader, who could garner great public support and sweep to power. They saw that Jesus could be that liberator. That's why many people gathered to cheer on Jesus as he entered Jerusalem, Shouting Hosanna, blessed is the He who comes in the name of the Lord." Would this be the moment? They could imagine how it would happen, how he would bring the people together and challenge the authority of the Romans and the Temple elite themselves.

And who would have made up the crowd on that Palm Sunday? His followers, by those he had preached to, healed, released; those whose lives had been transformed. These were people who'd been used to exclusion and rejection – lepers, the demon-possessed, the poor, the Gentiles, women, and he included them. Gave them value and dignity. He broke the social boundaries by eating with them. He demonstrated that they mattered to God. On that Palm Sunday, desperate for change and hope they gathered to acclaim him and herald him as King.

And of course, we know the story. Jesus fearlessly challenged the temple authorities and revealed their true colours. And we all know what bullies and dictators do when challenged in such a way. They seek to silence their opponents. All that week the temple elite waited for an opportunity to arrest him, to catch him out. But they couldn't act, for fear of the crowds, who loved him. It was only through the collusion of one of Jesus' closest friends, through his betrayal that they were able to act, arresting and sentencing him to death while the city slept. His crime! By the time people they were aware of anything happening it was too late, his fate was sealed. The liberator was killed by the oppressors, the dream had died. Hope had gone.

I've mentioned this in past years, because it's important to realise that for Jesus' followers, his death was an utter tragedy. They were not expecting a happy ending. There was no one waiting for him to reappear on the Sunday morning. There was no welcoming committee. There were the three women, the only ones to stay by Jesus' side as he was crucified –

Mary Magdalene, Mary the mother of James, and Salome bought spices so that they might go to anoint Jesus' body. Very early on the first day of the week, just after sunrise, they were on their way to the tomb and they asked each other, 'Who will roll the stone away from the entrance of the tomb?'
(Mark 16:1-3)

Their main concern is that they won't be able to get into the tomb to anoint the body. There's nothing else on their mind. However, the stone is rolled away, Jesus' body has gone, and a man dressed in white is there. He has the most extraordinary message.

'Don't be alarmed,' he said. 'You are looking for Jesus the Nazarene, who was crucified. He has risen! He is not here. See the place where they laid him. But go, tell his disciples and Peter, "He is going ahead of you into Galilee. There you will see him, just as he told you."'
(vv.6-7)

This news, this announcement, changes everything, but it doesn't make immediate sense for the women – they're still spinning. *"Trembling and bewildered, the women went out and fled from the tomb. They said nothing to anyone, because they were afraid"* (v.8).

And that's how the Gospel account in Mark ends. Bewilderment and fear. It is only dissipated when they meet with the risen Jesus and things begin to make sense.

You see, the thing is, Jesus was the Messiah, the liberator, and yet the Romans remained in power for the next 400 or so years. Things actually got worse for Jews in Israel in AD66-70 when a rebellion was crushed and the temple was destroyed. So, what was it all about?

Jesus did come to be the liberator. He was the promised Messiah, but he wasn't concerned with the powers and authorities. He had much bigger fish to fry. And this is relevant to us. Jesus came to be our liberator. He came to liberate us from the things that weigh us down. He came to break the chains that bind us.

The biggest enemy was **death**. Fear of death was and is a great weapon in the hands of the Romans and totalitarian regimes today. The idea that this life is all there is can be a weapon used to enslave and control many people. We still fear death today. We see this in the way that there is a desperate quest to prolong life, even if the quality of life that people experience is poor, we'd rather that than face our own death of the death of a loved one. We mask our fear of death by our folk religion, when we console ourselves that our lost loved ones are somewhere up there now, enjoying their favourite hobby.

So, death is our biggest enemy. And fear of death weighs many down.

What are the other things that can oppress us?

Rejection ... some of us experienced this at a very young age, and we still bear the weight of that today.

Bitterness ... we've been hurt in the past, and we've not been able to let go of this.

Sin ... there's stuff we've done or we're doing, that's wrong, even if we won't admit it.

Guilt ... we've done things in the past of which we're deeply ashamed, and we feel God possibly couldn't forgive us.

Fear/Anxiety ... we can't necessarily pin down why, but we're so scared and it cripples us.

These things can weigh us down so much. Some of us carry more than one of these things.

Jesus came to bring freedom, to bring liberation from the things that bind us.

He comes to us, and on the cross he takes the rejection, bitterness, guilt, fear, our sin, our fear, upon himself. He takes it, bears the weight of it himself, and then through the resurrection, he destroys it, replacing it.

Jesus's resurrection means that we don't need to fear death any more. And when we don't fear death any more, no one can hold any power over us. The resurrection destroys death and brings life.

Where we've been rejected, the resurrection declares that we are chosen.

Where there is bitterness and unforgiveness, Jesus brings power to forgive.

Where there is sin, Jesus brings purity

Where we feel guilt, he declares us innocent.

Where there is fear, Jesus can make us fearless.

The resurrection changes everything. Jesus is the liberator, the breaker of chains. We don't need to carry these things around any more. Jesus came to bring us life and hope.

What oppresses you today? Why not let Jesus the liberator come and set you free?

New Life, new Hope – John 20:1-18 (Easter Sunday Sunrise Sermon 2019)

This morning I want to share a simple message; it's about hope that springs out of hopelessness; of joy that springs from despair; about a tender God who loves us and knows us by name. It's the greatest story ever told – the Easter story that allows us to hope again. It's a big story – about the victory of this man Jesus over sin and death, but it's so much more than that; it's about the restoration of broken people and that's what I want to focus on this morning. For I believe there are people who need to hear such a story.

What must it have been like for Mary Magdalene as she made her way to Jesus' tomb that Sunday morning? Had she slept at all since we last saw her, when she watched Jesus being laid to rest by Joseph of Arimathea and Nicodemus? Or had she simply wept; bereft and lost? The man she watched being brutally crucified on that awful Friday was not simply any other man: he was the one on whom she and many others had pinned their hopes.

Before he came along, she was nothing – an outcast, plagued by seven demons; evil spirits that raged inside her – voices she neither recognised nor wanted to recognise. They wouldn't leave her alone. And then Jesus released her; he allowed her to hope again. So she followed him and witnessed incredible things. His amazing teaching was accompanied by incredible miracles: he healed the sick, cast out demons and even raised the dead. Amazing. Surely this man was the Messiah – the promised king who would rescue the Jewish people from all of their oppressors. As time passed, her hopes grew – hers and all of the others. Only last week he entered Jerusalem riding on a donkey as the crowds shouted, "Hosanna to the Son of David! Blessed is he who comes in the name of the Lord!"

158

The excitement grew ... and then ... and then ... she could scarcely believe it ... it all went horribly wrong. The reports came on Friday morning that he had been arrested and the next thing she knew she was watching him die. Crucifixion was an awful thing, but it was even worse when the man being crucified was the man you'd loved and on whom you'd pinned all your hopes. People mocked him, saying that he should save himself if he were the Son of God – and she hoped that he'd do just that – after all, she knew he had the power to. And she continued hoping, but that hope got smaller and smaller the shallower his breathing got. And then finally, he breathed his last with a final cry, "It is finished" and her hope had gone. She was devastated. It was all over.

We mustn't forget that when Mary makes her way to the tomb on that Sunday morning that she does not expect a happy ending. She expects to encounter Jesus' corpse. She expects to be able to serve him one last time. But the stone's been moved. Jesus' body is no longer there. As if Jesus hadn't undergone enough already, now his body has been stolen. It adds insult to awful injury. She runs to tell Simon Peter and the disciple Jesus loved, saying, "They have taken the Lord out of the tomb, and we don't know where they have put him!"

Impulsive Peter and the other disciple run off to check out her story. She is left behind, bereft. Now she weeps, not simply because Jesus is dead, but they have stolen his body. The one thing that had been left to her – the simple act of giving his body the treatment he deserves – even that has been taken away from her. She's probably reeling from everything that has happened to and stumbles her way back to the tomb. Why? Because she probably doesn't have anywhere else to go. I wonder if you have experienced that. Perhaps when someone you love has died, you find yourself in their room – even though you know they won't be coming back, you feel closer to them somehow. That's what Mary does – she goes back to the tomb, weeping fresh tears. And then something very unexpected happens,

> *Now Mary stood outside the tomb crying. As she wept, she bent over to look into the tomb and saw two angels in white, seated where Jesus' body had been, one at the head and the other at the foot.*
> *They asked her, "Woman, why are you crying?"*
> *"They have taken my Lord away," she said, "and I don't know where they have put him."*
> (vv.11-13)

You can hear the sorrow in her voice, can't you? "They have taken my Lord away and I don't know where they have put him."

She does not seem to see the angels; all she can think about is the fact her Lord's body has gone. The devastation experienced on the Friday has been compounded by shock that someone would steal Jesus' body and then probably bewilderment at this latest development.

Let's pause there and rest in the sense of bewilderment, shock and despair. Because we know the end of the story, we gloss over the devastation that probably swept over Mary. But I think that to do so is to a mistake. There is a myth that Christian experience is all hunky dory; that once we come to faith in Jesus, everything will be easy and that we will always be joyful.

We expect that every day will be like Easter, but then awful things happen. Someone we love falls ill and then, despite our fervent prayers, they die. We experience the bitterness of divorce; our children deny the faith that is at the centre of our very beings. Whatever it is, we feel something like Mary did – hurting, lost, despairing and angry. It seems like too many days are like that awful Friday, or like that moment we've just paused on that Easter morning before the penny drops.

This morning I feel that I have to say one thing – that experience of brokenness and despair that you are going through; it's ok to feel like that. Just dip in the Psalms and you'll see that there is a lot of anger and despair around. You're not abnormal. If you want to shout at God, then that's ok – if you find yourself constantly asking "WHY", that's ok too – God knows. I'll say that again – he knows.

But that needn't be the end of the end of the story. God doesn't want to leave you like that. Mary Magdalene was in the depths of despair, but that changed.

Let's re-join the story, to see how … Suddenly she sees someone in the corner of her eye – perhaps he could help. She doesn't realise that it's Jesus. She wouldn't be able to see him properly anyway, her eyes are so blurred by tears.

> *He asked her, "Woman, why are you crying? Who is it you are looking for?" Thinking he was the gardener, she said, "Sir, if you have carried him away, tell me where you have put him, and I will get him."* (v.15)

Let's pause there again. The first thing Jesus does is to ask Mary why she's crying. Of course, he knows already, but he wants her to tell him, for her to allow him to help.

And I believe that today, he is asking us the same question. If there is something troubling you, that causes you an ache in your heart, Jesus knows it already, but he longs for you to share it with him. Why are you crying? Why are you hurting?

Let's just be quiet for a moment and name that in our hearts – because Jesus wants to share our burdens, to listen to our pain.

Let's go back to the passage again. Mary thinks that Jesus is the gardener, so she asks him if he'd moved the body and if so, where it was. Even though he's standing there in front of her, Mary's grief blinds her to his true identity.

But then everything changes with one word. "Mary."

That's the moment the penny drops. Mary realises who this man is – that the man who'd set her free from those demons, had taught incredible things and done wonderful works and who she'd watched die just two days previously; this is the man who wonderfully, incredibly, but truly, is alive. Jesus is alive!

What makes her come to this realisation? What makes the penny drop? I think it's the way Jesus speaks to her, as well as the fact he calls her by name. He is alive, and because of that, Mary can hope again. No wonder she holds onto him, no wonder she rushes off to her disciples, proclaiming the wonderful news, "I have seen the Lord!"

Jesus is alive. And that is why we can hope again. He wants us to tell him why we're hurting, he wants to share our burdens.

He calls us by name, because he wants us to see and to grow to understand who he really is. He is the risen Lord Jesus, who experienced the most incredible suffering that none of us will ever fully understand, but then he overcame the greatest enemies, sin and death. He is the reason we can hope.

He is Jesus, who is God in human form, who loved the world so much that he lived a fully human life, experiencing every emotion and experience, who died on the cross, but amazingly rose from the dead, showing us that he is king over sin, suffering and death – that he has overcome them all, and that he is Lord of life.

It is the same Jesus who knows us each by name, who knows everything we are going through and wants to meet us in the midst of our suffering and set us free. He is with us in our darkest hour and can bring us strength, comfort, peace and hope – hope that the pain and sorrow will end forever, and be replaced by unending and unfailing joy and peace.

This is Jesus, who restores us and brings hope out of despair.

If you don't yet have this life-changing, hope-filling relationship with Jesus, Easter is a great time to begin or renew this transforming relationship. Speak to me afterwards if you want to know more.

This is Jesus. He is risen. He is alive. Alleluia!

<u>Keeping the Faith – Luke 24:1-12, 1 Corinthians 15:1-8, 12-22 (Easter Sunday Sunrise Sermon 2021)</u>

One of the delights of being a dad is reading stories. Bedtime has always been one of my favourite times of the day, because it's story time. Sometimes when the girls were younger, we manage to sneak in a quick time for a cuddle and a read first thing in the morning if I was awake enough. I read through the Chronicles of Narnia with both of my daughters and it was wonderful doing so. In our journey through the Chronicles we encountered many interesting characters, perhaps none more curious than Puddleglum, in the *Silver Chair*. He accompanies Eustace and Jill in the mission Aslan gave them to find the lost prince of Narnia, Rilian. Their quest takes them to a city deep underground, ruled by the Lady of the Green Kirtle, also known as the Witch. There they discover the lost prince who'd been bound by the Witch's enchantments. They break the spell but soon afterwards she tries to bewitch them, putting green powder on a fire that lets off a sweet smell and plays music. She speaks in a sweet, quiet voice, casting doubt on all that they have seen and experienced – seeking to convince them that there is no Narnia, Overworld, sun, or even, Aslan – no other reality apart from the Underworld in which they're trapped.

> "'Tis a pretty make-believe … though, to say truth, it would suit you all better if you were younger. … There is no Narnia, no Overworld, no sky, no sun, no Aslan. And now, to bed all. And let us begin a wiser life tomorrow. But, first, to bed; to sleep; deep sleep, soft pillows, sleep without foolish dreams."

Just a couple of weeks ago we all completed the census. There was an article in the Guardian that noted that for the first time less than half of Britons are likely to tick "Christian" this year.

164

It will, the article says, cement the fact that we are a post-Christian society – it quotes, Professor Abby Day who says, "Post-Christians are motivated by ethics concerning gender and sexual equality, social justice, climate change and compassion. The churches failed to deliver on those moral issues and so lost moral authority. Today's younger generations have a different sense of soul, meaning and morality, and it's one that rejects the church's record of abuse, racism, homophobia and sexism." And the article notes that less than 1% people attend a Church of England church – and a third of these are over 70. It's depressing isn't it – especially when coupled with discouraging headlines like that on the BBC a few years ago that proclaimed, "Resurrection did not happen, say a quarter of Christians" which cited a poll that said that exactly half of all people surveyed didn't believe in the resurrection at all. Reverend Lorraine Cavanagh, speaking on behalf of Modern Church, says,

> "Science, but also intellectual and philosophical thought has progressed. … So to ask an adult to believe in the resurrection the way they did when they were at Sunday school simply won't do and that's true of much of the key elements of the Christian faith."

I don't know how you react to such headlines. They can be so discouraging can't they. The implication is clear – belief in God is on the decline. Christianity is not for grown ups. As for belief in the resurrection, grown-up Christians have got over that too. Thinking about it, it's remarkable how much the words of Reverend Cavanagh echo the words of the Witch. A belief in the resurrection she says, is pretty make believe – and would suit you all better if you were younger. The Christians from previous generations were more gullible than we are today. We're more educated. We know better. This has an impact, doesn't it? When these sorts of opinions are expressed possibly in our family circles, or among our friends or colleagues, perhaps we feel silly, perhaps we doubt ourselves. These events were so long ago, after all, weren't they? Maybe they're right, after all? And as for life after death, that's just a nice belief isn't it – comforting – a crutch, nothing more. We all know, grown up people do, anyway, that this life is all there is. After all, there's no concrete proof – not in the way that we understand it, anyway. There aren't many stories of people experiencing resurrection these days, are there, after all? Maybe they're right. Maybe it's just a story to make us feel better ... And then we listen to the other voices that tell us we can't really rely on the writers of the Bible anyway, these stories were edited much later ...

And the sickly fumes of these voices, so soothing, so deceptive gradually wear us down. The seeds of doubt are sown. And then we begin to doubt our own experiences of God, when we've sensed God guiding and speaking to us, when we've sensed his presence. Perhaps they're not real either? Just our imagination – as if wishing made it so.

These voices threaten to overwhelm us. And they sound logical don't they, after all, we all know that dead men don't rise from the dead. We fight to hold onto our faith in Jesus, while the voice speaks to us and says that he was a story too – or if he were real, he was no more than a man. It all seems so convincing, doesn't it ... and if a poll tells us that there are a significant proportion of Christians who don't believe in the resurrection – well, maybe they're right ...

And we see those voices coming out in the Bible accounts themselves, don't we? In Luke's account of the resurrection, when Mary and her companions have met with the angel and been told that Jesus has risen, the disciples ridicule them – *"But they did not believe the women, because their words seemed to them like nonsense"* (Luke 24:11) and later on, the air of disbelief continues as the two disciples trudge towards Emmaus –

"some of our women amazed us. They went to the tomb early this morning but didn't find his body. They came and told us that they had seen a vision of angels, who said he was alive. Then some of our companions went to the tomb and found it just as the women had said, but they did not see Jesus.'
(vv.22-24).

You'd expect there to be an air of faith and expectation, but there isn't. Instead, there is simply an air of confusion, doubt, bewilderment. The women must be deluded. After all, dead men don't rise.

And yet, and yet, and yet ...

Deep in Underworld, it seems as if the witch has won. The four people have fallen under her spell. But then, Puddleglum shakes himself and stamps out the fire, breaking the spell. The smell went, which "instantly made everyone's brain far clearer. The Prince and the children held up their heads again and opened their eyes."

Then Puddleglum spoke ...

One word, Ma'am," he said, coming back from the fire; limping, because of the pain. "One word. All you've been saying is quite right, I shouldn't wonder. I'm a chap who always liked to know the worst and then put the best face I can on it. So I won't deny any of what you said. But there's one more thing to be said, even so. Suppose we have only dreamed, or made up, all those things-trees and grass and sun and moon and stars and Aslan himself. Suppose we have. Then all I can say is that, in that case, the made-up things seem a good deal more important than the real ones. Suppose this black pit of a kingdom of yours is the only world. Well, it strikes me as a pretty poor one. And that's a funny thing, when you come to think of it. We're just babies making up a game, if you're right. But four babies playing a game can make a play-world which licks your real world hollow. That's why I'm going to stand by the play world. I'm on Aslan's side even if there isn't any Aslan to lead it. I'm going to live as like a Narnian as I can even if there isn't any Narnia. So, thanking you kindly for our supper, if these two gentlemen and the young lady are ready, we're leaving your court at once and setting out in the dark to spend our lives looking for Overland. Not that our lives will be very long, I should think; but that's a small loss if the world's as dull a place as you say.

I won't go into details of what happens next, but suffice to say, the spell is broken and the four companions are able to see the Witch's true nature – she transforms into a serpent – and they discover that her words are all lies. There is a world above, there is a Narnia, there is a sun, … there is Aslan.

I think there's so much we can learn from Puddleglum. If the dominant voices in our increasingly secular, so-called more grown-up society are right, there is no life beyond the one we see. There is no long-term hope, the most important thing I can do in life is look after those people close to me, everyone else can look after themselves. And yet, this pandemic that we've been thrust into has led people to question their assumptions about life and death.

Forgive me if I speak against a fellow vicar, but Ms Cavanagh of Modern Church, is speaking nonsense. If she's right and that the resurrection didn't really happen, Christianity is utterly, completely pointless, based on a lie that's taken in millions of people. St Paul himself puts it in 1 Corinthians 15,

But if it is preached that Christ has been raised from the dead, how can some of you say that there is no resurrection of the dead? If there is no resurrection of the dead, then not even Christ has been raised. And if Christ has not been raised, our preaching is useless and so is your faith. More than that, we are then found to be false witnesses about God, for we have testified about God that he raised Christ from the dead. But he did not raise him if in fact the dead are not raised. For if the dead are not raised, then Christ has not been

raised either. And if Christ has not been raised, your faith is futile; you are still in your sins. Then those also who have fallen asleep in Christ are lost. If only for this life we have hope in Christ, we are of all people most to be pitied.
(vv.12-19)

People like Lorraine Cavanagh speak as if people have only recently been questioning the reality of the resurrection. Actually, they were doing that when St Paul was writing, only 20 or so years after Jesus' death and resurrection. And Paul is clear. Without the resurrection, the Christian faith is a complete and utter waste of time.

Indulge me for a moment. What if the resurrection did happen? What if the tomb were empty on that third day? What if? What if?

Because Paul, although he is well aware of the claims that the resurrection didn't happen, he continues …

But Christ has indeed been raised from the dead, the firstfruits of those who have fallen asleep. For since death came through a man, the resurrection of the dead comes also through a man. For as in Adam all die, so in Christ all will be made alive.
(vv.20-22)

If the resurrection happened, it changes everything. I mean, *everything*. It doesn't just mean that we have hope that once we die there will be heaven waiting for us, whatever that may look like. But it means life today, here and now, takes on a completely different meaning and purpose. Puddleglum gets that. It impacts the way we live here and now. It means that we pray and live in such a way that God's kingdom might come wherever we are, living in such a way to make our bit of a world a better place. Why? Because if Jesus' resurrection really happened, then we can also trust Jesus' words when he tells us that what matters most is that we love God and our neighbour, not that we love and care for ourselves. This is why his life led to the cross and ours should as well. Christ died to self and called us to go and do likewise because the new creation cannot dawn if we're still focused on self. Rather than taking care of ourselves first and then going out into the world to do the work of the Kingdom, the work of the Kingdom begins by dying to self first and then continually putting the needs of others before our own.

The resurrection changes everything for today as well as tomorrow. It's not an escape plan – a one way ticket to eternity. Instead, it's a call to participate in the building of a new world, in the bringing of heaven to earth. This is the sort of faith that Puddleglum is professing. One which tries to live out the hope he believes in, rather than waiting for the day when it might come to pass.

Imagine what the Church and the world would be like if we had faith like Puddleglum.

Imagine what might happen if our faith wasn't just about believing the right things so we can get out of here and on our way to heaven.

Imagine what would happen if, instead, our focus was on caring for others and transforming the here and now.

And as for those arguments with those who deny the reality of the resurrection, they also would become irrelevant if all Christians begin to start living like Jesus, whether or not God is real and whether or not that tomb is empty, because this world would be completely transformed. So if we struggle with doubts, let's take a leaf out of Puddleglum's book anyway.

Having said all this, I believe in the resurrection with every fibre of my being. I believe that when Mary Magdalene went to the tomb that Sunday morning, she did find it empty and then met with the risen Lord Jesus face to face having previously mistaken him to be the gardener. I believe there is good evidence for it as a historical event. Actually, the BBC article was deceptive. The vast majority of practicing

Christians – over 90% – believe in the resurrection – and they include grown-ups.

I believe I've experienced the power of the risen Jesus in my life and witnessed it in this church community, but I can't prove any of this – and I don't think I ever will. But I wonder whether it's time to stop worrying about it, and live out the truth that I believe. Because, let's face it, the reality in which there is a God who loved the world so much that he sent his Son to live and become the best possible role model, and then to die for it as the greatest imaginable act of self-sacrifice, and that through this very same man's resurrection he gave the world the lifeline it so desperately needed, and in turn he encouraged all those who have faith in him to follow his example and to love each other and the world to the point of sacrifice – this reality far surpasses any other. It's a reality I would die for – and in the meantime, want to live for with every part of my being. Are you with me? And when we live like this, then the risen Lord Jesus is present among us, and no one will be able to hide his reality.

Alleluia, the Lord is risen.
He is risen indeed. Alleluia.

From Death to Life - 1 Corinthians 15:1-8; 19-26, 55-58, Matthew 28:1-10 (Easter Sunday Sunrise Sermon 2022)

I have to confess that over the past few months my faith has taken a bit of a kicking. Coming to terms with the premature death of someone within our church from cancer has been a really difficult thing to do. It was hard to see the good in it; that someone could suffer so much and then, when she died, leave behind a mum, partner, young daughters and friends – it didn't make sense. If God is able to heal, why didn't he? And on a global scale we've watched on helplessly as the people of Ukraine have been besieged by war; on top of the terrible destruction wrought on cities, with billions of pounds worth of damage done, grim evidence has been uncovered of terrible atrocities, with civilians being treated horrifically. It's grim, isn't it? How do we make sense of a God who is good when there is such suffering? Where do we look for comfort, solace, hope?

We look to the dawn of this very day when the disciples were waking up, desperately hoping that the events of two days previously were a terrible dream. Of course, they weren't. When they woke up, Jesus was still dead, and they no longer had their leader with them. What were they to do now? After all, they'd always followed Jesus. He'd known what to do. Whether it was to tour around the towns and villages of Galilee, or to go down to Jerusalem, Jesus would lead them, teach them, guide them. But he was gone now, arrested and killed by the Romans, at the behest of the religious leaders. Surely it wasn't safe for them either. So, the men stayed hidden, afraid for their lives, while the women kept themselves busy. Many women *"had followed Jesus from Galilee to care for his needs"* (27:55). While most of the disciples had scattered after Jesus's arrest, they had been present at the cross, watching from a distance. Mary Magdalene and Jesus's mother were standing at the foot of the cross, they'd seen him die, watched his body being taken down from the cross and they watched him being buried. They'd been forced to do nothing on the Sabbath day, but as soon as they were able, at dawn, they went to the tomb. Why? Well, according to John's Gospel they went to the tomb to anoint his body burial - typical of those whose role has been to care for Jesus's needs, and so they had one final chance to do this, Here, though, we're simply told that they went to look at the tomb; in the same way that we visit a cemetery or sit in their room, because we feel closer to the loved one who we've lost, perhaps they wanted to feel closer to Jesus somehow. Either way, they were grief-stricken, full of questions, in a state of shock. And soon, added to the grief would come fear. An angel of the Lord appeared, an earthquake struck, leaving guards quaking and the women dumfounded, terrified, wondering what on earth was going on.

And before we rush onto the next bit, the happy ending, let's take a breath. Grief, shock, fear. This is the reality for the women on that morning and for the disciples who are in Jerusalem somewhere hiding. Perhaps we feel that too. I know I have in these past months – grief once I realised that she was going to die, that the miracle I had prayed for and almost expected was now not going to happen, shock and disbelief when the news came that she had died, and, I confess to you, fear. Fear – what if heaven isn't waiting for us when we die? What if we're not right about this? I wonder if you can relate to that. I wonder if you're in a place where fear, grief and shock is a reality for you. You're not alone. The disciples experienced that, the two Marys experienced that and, you know what, and this is absolutely crucial for us, this is the thing that gives us most hope – Jesus felt that too. On that Thursday night in Gethsemane, he was plagued by grief at the prospect of the horror that awaited him and of the prospect of being parted from his disciples – friends whom he'd loved. I believe there would have been some fear too – fear of just how awful his suffering would be – he knew what the Romans could do, after all, and possibly fear that what if he wasn't who he believed he was. What if his death would end in just that – his death?

So, some of us simply need to know that the dark path we're walking, we're not alone. The disciples walked that path, but Jesus did too. There's great comfort in that, as Ali once reflected, "Holy week has a fresh meaning for me this year, as I walk through the events of history hand in hand with Jesus, giving him my fear and my pain. Knowing he completely understands."

The events of Holy Week, with all their darkness – the grief, shock, fear, tell us that Jesus completely understands. Isn't that amazing.

But that's not where it ends. Jesus meets us in that place but he doesn't leave us there. We see this as the events of that extraordinary Sunday morning unfold.

> *The angel said to the women, "Do not be afraid, for I know that you are looking for Jesus, who was crucified. He is not here; he has risen, just as he said. Come and see the place where he lay. Then go quickly and tell his disciples: 'He has risen from the dead and is going ahead of you into Galilee. There you will see him.' Now I have told you."*
> *So the women hurried away from the tomb, afraid yet filled with joy, and ran to tell his disciples.*
> (Matthew 28:5-8)

Hear the angel's message. He is not here – he is risen <u>just as he said.</u> He was crucified – he went through all that pain, all that suffering. He died. He was buried, but now he is alive – as he said he would be. And again, as the angel clearly gets that the women must be reeling, as he commissions the women – "he has risen from the dead" – go and tell his disciples.

This message that the women are given changes everything. No wonder they're full of joy.

And then, they meet Jesus face to face…

Suddenly Jesus met them. "Greetings," he said. They came to him, clasped his feet and worshiped him. Then Jesus said to them, "Do not be afraid. Go and tell my brothers to go to Galilee; there they will see me."
(vv.9-10)

The two women came to the tomb, broken-hearted, full of grief, fear, shock and not really knowing what to do. But everything has changed. They're full of joy and they've been given new purpose and new hope.

What they had just heard had changed everything – not just for them but for everyone everywhere who has ever lived. The empty tomb changes everything. As Tom Wright summarises,

Something had happened, something that had not only changed the women's hearts but had torn a hole in normal history. … This event had changed the world for ever. … Jesus is revealed as the one through whom death itself is defeated.[*]

And this is what us to find comfort and hope in this morning.

Death itself has been defeated. This changes everything. It changes how we face suffering, even cancer.

In his book, *God on Mute*, Pete Greig describes a woman, Margaret Lee, who suffered from throat cancer. She was greeted by people who had such sympathy for her condition and suffering. Surely, this cancer was the worst thing imaginable.

---

[*] Tom Wright, *Matthew for Everyone*, SPCK

Margaret soon got so used to this well-meaning assessment of her situation that she wrote her standard response on a piece of scrap paper. I think it's probably one of the most courageous declarations of faith in Jesus that I have ever seen.

"This is not the worst thing to ever happen! Cancer is so limited. It cannot cripple love, shatter hope, corrode faith, eat away peace, destroy confidence, kill friendship, shut out memories, silence courage, quench the Spirit, or lessen the power of Jesus."[*]

Isn't that extraordinary?

Tim Keller, an author, former pastor and theologian was told in 2020 that he had terminal pancreatic cancer – when he found out it was a kind of death. In an interview in the *New York Times* earlier this week, he reflected how it's changed things for him since his diagnosis. Most of all, he realised how much more he needed to grow in his faith –

My experience of his presence and his love was going to have to double, triple, quintuple or I wouldn't make it.[†]

This meant investing time in prayer, worshipping with the church family, reading the Scriptures –

Learning how to take what he's read in the Bible and screw it down into his heart till it catches fire. …
I pray more often, but I also do it more longingly. And what's really amazing is that when you know you've got to have more

---

[*] Pete Greig, *God on Mute: Engaging the Silence of Unanswered Prayer*, David C. Cook (2022)
[†] "Opinion | Timothy Keller on Hope Amidst Terminal Cancer," *New York Times,* 10 April 2022,
https://www.nytimes.com/2022/04/10/opinion/timothy-keller-cancer-easter.html

of God — because there's really no alternative — to our surprise, there is more of God to be gotten.

And then he speaks about hope. When asked, where do you find hope? What hope do you offer to others?

He replies …

> If the resurrection of Jesus Christ really happened, then ultimately, God is going to put everything right. Suffering is going to go away. Evil is going to go away. Death is going to go away. Aging is going to go away. Pancreatic cancer is going to go away. Now if the resurrection of Jesus Christ did not happen, then I guess all bets are off. But if it actually happened, then there's all the hope in the world. …
>
> "Holy Week gives you both death and resurrection. They don't make any sense apart. You can't have the joy of resurrection unless you've gone through a death, and death without resurrection is just hopeless. Essentially, the death/resurrection motif or pattern is absolutely at the heart of what it means to live a Christian life. And actually everything in life is like that. With any kind of suffering, if I respond to it by looking to God in faith, suffering drives me like a nail deeper into God's love, which is what cancer has done for me.
>
> I do think that the great thing about cancer is that Easter does mean a whole lot more because I look at Easter and I say, "Because of this, I can face anything." In the past, I thought of Easter as a kind of optimistic, upbeat way of thinking about life. And now I see that Easter is a universal solvent. It can eat through any fear, any anger and despair. I see it as more powerful than ever before."

Easter did happen. The Resurrection is a reality, as Paul declares in 1 Corinthians 15 –

> *"Christ died for our sins according to the Scriptures, [4] … he was buried, … he was raised on the third day according to the Scriptures, [5] and that he appeared to Cephas,[k] and then to the Twelve."*

177

(vv.3-5)

As he says, this is of "first importance" – this changes everything. As he later proclaims

> *'Where, O death, is your victory?*
> *Where, O death, is your sting?'*
> *The sting of death is sin, and the power of sin is the law. But thanks be to God! He gives us the victory through our Lord Jesus Christ.*
> (vv.55-57)

So, in the meantime what do we do?

Last Sunday evening, I shared about a picture that I was given - it was of walking boots caked in mud. As the mud accumulates on the boots it gets harder to walk. The person who shared, without knowing anything of our circumstances, said that she sensed life had felt like that for me. She said that she felt that the mud was hardening and would break off - that we'd walk free once more. The mud is all the rubbish we've been through. The resurrection means Jesus has power to break down it off. The power of death has been destroyed, because he is risen, just as he said. There is unending, undying, unquenchable hope. Let's cling to that hope - and let's heed Pauls words in 1 Corinthians 15

> *Therefore, my dear brothers and sisters, stand firm. Let nothing move you. Always give yourselves fully to the work of the Lord, because you know that your labour in the Lord is not in vain.*
> (v.58)

The Road to Hope – Luke 24:13-35 (The Sunday after Easter)

"We had hoped"

Three words that express the devastation of loss.

"We had hoped"

Three words that express utter disappointment and perhaps even disillusionment.

These three words are uttered by two disciples, one of whom is named as Cleopas – who may have been Jesus' maternal uncle – who are walking away from Jerusalem to Emmaus. Weary with exhaustion and grief, their steps are heavy and their heads are bowed. They're joined by a mysterious companion and all they can talk about is their experience over the past few days and their disbelief that the one they had served and followed for a couple of years was dead. You can hear the grief in their voices as they lament to their strange companion:

> *"Jesus of Nazareth … was a prophet, powerful in word and deed before God and all the people. The chief priests and our rulers handed him over to be sentenced to death, and they crucified him; but we had hoped that he was the one who was going to redeem Israel."*
> (vv.19-21)

"We had hoped."

Their hopes for a bright future have been dashed. It's all over now.

What is the first thing their new companion does? Having approached them and drawn alongside them, he asks them, "What are you discussing together as you walk along?" – or, in short, "what's up? What's on your hearts?" The first thing he does is listen.

We know who their new companion is, we're in on the secret. The Lord Jesus knows exactly what's up. They don't need to tell him, but he asks anyway. Why? Because he wants them to tell him, for them to allow him to help.

And I believe that today, he is asking us the same question. If there is something troubling you, that causes you an ache in your heart, Jesus knows it already, but he longs for you to share it with him. What's up? What's on your heart?

Let's just be quiet for a moment and name that in our hearts – because Jesus wants to share our burdens, to listen to our pain. Perhaps you might begin by saying to Jesus, "We had hoped …" "I had hoped … " and fill in the gap yourself.

Of course we know the end of the story; that the disciples' strange companion is Jesus, but they don't know that – all they know is that they have someone to listen to them. And they pour out their hearts to him. But the wonderful truth is that it is Jesus himself who's listening to them. The disciples are so clouded by grief that they don't believe the women's story that Jesus is alive – even though the other disciples have corroborated their account of the empty tomb.

Why does Jesus wait to reveal himself to the disciples? Why does he never tell them who he was, only allowing his teaching and his actions to speak for themselves through breaking the bread? Is it that actions speak louder than words? That he knows that the wonder of that moment of realization that would come as he broke the bread, as they discover the truth that it's him – and that he's alive – for themselves would surpass being told straight away? Perhaps he knows that there are some things we need to discover for ourselves? Is it because he delights to surprise people?

I believe that the truth lies in all of these. We have a God who delights in surprising us. I know that some of us will be saying a hearty "amen" at this point!

We have a God who delights in bringing life out of death, hope out of hopelessness and light out of darkness. We have a God who shows us his love and care for us through his actions as well as his words. And I think we can testify to that in our church community. Though the last few years have been a struggle in varying ways, we're coming through and I believe we're actually stronger. The way we have come together through caring for those among us who have been suffering in different ways has been a great testimony to God's power working in and through us. I think a number of us who have experienced that suffering first-hand and have experienced renewed hope in spite of difficult circumstances. I trust, hope and pray that those of us who find themselves caught in the middle of this suffering will discover that new life and renewed hope for themselves.

Jesus and the Miraculous Catch of Fish – John 21:1-14

Have you ever really messed up or let someone down? I'm sure all of us had times when we've, quite frankly stuffed up. We'll all be familiar with that sense of shame and guilt. We'd all be aware of that feeling of not being able to face that person we've let down, especially if it's someone whom we love and respect. It'd be good to have this in mind as we look at our bible passage this morning.

We're with some of the disciples some time after Jesus' resurrection. He's already appeared to them twice in the upper room, as we saw last week, now some of them are back in Galilee, where the adventure began. Lots has happened since they were last at the shore of this lake. And you get the impression that they don't really know what to do. They're a bit lost. Since Jesus, their leader, was taken away from them, they've been left like a ship without a rudder. What should they do now? So Peter, typically, the leader of the bunch, makes a suggestion – let's go fishing. He's been told by Jesus to wait to be clothed with power from on high, doesn't have a clue what that means – hates to wait for anything anyway, so decides he's going to do something. He wants to get on with life, and it seems sensible to go back to the old life – after all, they have responsibilities and families to look after, money to earn, people to feed. Catching fish seems like a good idea. After all, that's what they are – they're fishermen. They know the sea, they know where to find fish. *"I'm going out to fish,"* *Simon Peter told them, and they said, "We'll go with you."* (v.3)

But it doesn't go to plan – *"So they went out and got into the boat, but that night they caught nothing."* (v.3) All night, no fish. How futile! Experienced fishermen know that you have the best chance of catching fish in the night time.

They're weary, possibly a little frustrated – definitely ready for food and rest – and it's at that moment that Jesus appears. They don't know it's him at first. They soon do, because Jesus has a way of making himself known.

> *Early in the morning, Jesus stood on the shore, but the disciples did not realise that it was Jesus.*
> *He called out to them, "Friends, haven't you any fish?"*
> *"No," they answered.*
> *He said, "Throw your net on the right side of the boat and you will find some." When they did, they were unable to haul the net in because of the large number of fish.*
> *Then the disciple whom Jesus loved said to Peter, "It is the Lord!"*
> (vv.4-7)

As soon as this miracle takes place, they know for sure, in an instant, that it's the Lord. I wonder how Peter feels? Does anxiety and perhaps guilt bubble up in him? Does he have a flashback to those moments in the Garden when he struck out with his sword and then fled; those moments in the courtyard when he denied ever having known Jesus and when their gaze met before the cock crowed and he ran out weeping? The moment the disciples in Emmaus realised it was Jesus he disappeared; perhaps it would be easier for Peter if Jesus disappeared this time, but he doesn't; he waits for them on the shore. How would we feel if we were in Peter's shoes? Something like the feeling we have when we've let someone down and have to face that person again. How does Peter react? He could hide and hope Jesus hasn't seen him. But he doesn't. In Verse 7 we read, *"As soon as Simon Peter heard him say, "It is the Lord," he wrapped his outer garment around him (for he had taken it off) and jumped into the water."*

He longs to see Jesus again. He clearly has some unfinished business with him. So he impulsively grabs a cloak and leaps in the sea, leaving the others to do the hard work.

It's worth recalling that at the end of the previous chapter, Jesus gave his disciples a clear commission –

Jesus said, "Peace be with you! As the Father has sent me, I am sending you." And with that he breathed on them and said, "Receive the Holy Spirit."
(20:21-22)

As Tom Wright summarises,

They are to work for him, to be filled with God's breath and to be sent into the world as Jesus had been. But if they try to do it on their own, they will fail. They will toil all night and take nothing. The only way is to admit defeat, to listen afresh to Jesus' voice, and to do what he says. Then there is no knowing what they will achieve.[*]

God had given the disciples a clear commission and then they tried to make it happen in their own way, and in their own strength.

Haven't we all tried to do that at some stage in our lives? It doesn't often work out does it? We try and make things happen. Strive to do things in our own strength. We may have struggles with sin, or other issues that we wrestle with that we try to fight in our own strength. We try to be good enough for God, to make the grade. Whether at home, at church, at work, in your own life with God, we strive and strive and strive?

You know what Jesus says? Listen to my voice. Trust me – with all your worries and anxieties. Run like Peter towards me. Don't struggle and strive. Listen to me and do what I tell you.

There's another message we need to hear too – some of us strive to be good enough for God, to work and work and work for him, so that somehow we will be worthy. But Jesus

---

[*] Tom Wright, *John for Everyone*, SPCK

isn't really interested in that. He just wants to be with us. He wants to cook breakfast for us. Verse 9 says, *"When they landed, they saw a fire of burning coals there with fish on it, and some bread."* Jesus doesn't need the disciples' fish. He had a fire ready and waiting for them, with fish and bread. And he invites them bring some of their fish and join him:

> *"Jesus said to them, "Come and have breakfast." None of the disciples dared ask him, "Who are you?" They knew it was the Lord.* [13] *Jesus came, took the bread and gave it to them, and did the same with the fish.*
> (vv.12-13)

Some of us keep striving, because we don't really know, deep down, that Jesus loves us. That he likes us. We have this image of God as being a stern headmaster ready to punish us whenever we step out of line, but actually He loves us. Jesus wants to be good news for us. He wants our lives to be full of hope, he wants us to know that we can rest in him.

Adrian Plass, the Christian author and speaker, had the following reflections on this passage:

> Perhaps Jesus says to us, 'Look, if you were in a boat, and you suddenly saw me on the shore, would you jump in the water — sins and complications and all — and run as fast as you could towards me, simply because you love me? Would you sit beside the fire with me, share a bit of fish, and make a decision that you'll go and love people for me even though you are a grade one pillock? I don't expect you to be perfect, I want you to be obedient. Whose side are you on? Yours — or yours and mine?'
>
> I certainly have not got where I need to be yet, but I'll tell you this, I seriously think that I'm safer sitting on that beach with Jesus, eating fish and having a laugh and knowing I'm loved, than in many, many sections and enclaves of what we call the church, where so many brows are creased by worry about whether God loves them enough to put up with them in paradise. …

Every last little passionate push by the Holy Spirit is aimed is aimed at landing us, not in a swamp of questions and concerns and self-obsessed entrail examination but on a little beach beside a beautiful lake where we can find peace with a friend who will undoubtedly have a job for us to do.*

Jesus loves us. He speaks into our souls and tells us to come to him so that he can give us rest. His grace is sufficient for us; his power is made perfect in our weakness.

He wants us to stop trying so hard to get into his good books, because we are. He wants us to stop trying so hard with our projects and listen to what he wants and find that things will happen in his way and in his strength.

Will we get out of the boat and splash towards him? Will we allow him to share himself with us and cook us breakfast? Will we allow Jesus simply to love us?

---

* Adrian Plass and Jeff Lucas, *Seriously Funny 2: More Musings between Two Good Friends on Life, Love & God*, Authentic Media (2012)

New Hope, new Purpose – Luke 24:33-53

For the disciples on that Sunday morning, it was a day that began with grief and sadness, uncertainty, fear, exhaustion, confusion and hopelessness.

Grief and sadness – The Lord they had followed, their friend Jesus, who had given them such purpose and made them feel so loved had been taken away from them suddenly and brutally, killed in the prime of his life by people who were threatened by him.

Uncertainty - with Jesus dead, they wondered what they were going to do now.

Hopelessness – they'd believed Jesus was the answer to all their prayers, the one who would lead them and the whole nation to freedom. But that was all gone now. There was no hope for them now, not that they could see.

Fear – they believed the Jewish leaders who had killed Jesus would be after them too, so they hid and locked all the doors.

Exhaustion - I bet they hadn't slept much the past few nights since Jesus had been arrested.

Confusion – When the women returned with their news of the empty tomb and their reports of meeting angels the disciples simply didn't believe them – they thought the women were talking rubbish. They must have wondered what was going on.

The picture we are given on the morning of Easter Sunday is a bewildered, confused bunch of people. Even Peter, the leader of the disciples, who had run off to discover for himself that the tomb was empty – even he had no idea what was going on.

It sounds familiar doesn't it. Many of us have experienced these feelings – of uncertainty, sadness, confusion and fear – in the past month or so, as this coronavirus has changed our lives in ways we couldn't have possibly imagined just a couple of months ago. Perhaps we're struggling with these feelings at the moment. Perhaps we feel stuck in this moment and can't see a way out.

I don't believe Jesus wants us to stay stuck. I believe God wants to renew and restore us, to bring us new hope.

That's what Jesus did for the disciples. Last week we saw how two of the disciples had this strange encounter on the road to Emmaus with a man who turns out to be the risen Jesus himself, who revealed his true identity to them as he opened the Scriptures with them and shared a meal with them. Amazed, full of renewed hope they ran back to Jerusalem, to join the rest of the disciples, where they heard the amazing, unbelievable news that Jesus had indeed risen and appeared to Peter.

Peter had been on a rollercoaster ride of emotions hadn't he? Let's imagine what those days must have been like for him.

- - - -

Peter's Story

I didn't sleep a wink. I couldn't. I felt so awful. Sick in the pit of my stomach. Those words he had said to me kept going round my head. "Tonight, before the cock crows, you'll deny you've ever known me." I couldn't believe it! Me, Peter, the one he'd nicknamed Rocky, deny Jesus? I'd never deny Jesus. Never. As if I could. He was the man who had given me purpose. Life was so exciting when he was around. I'd made lots of mistakes, but he forgave every one – amazing really. How could I ever deny the man who'd turned my life upside down? Who'd allowed me to share in the greatest adventure ever? I couldn't!

But I did. Three times. Swore I didn't have the faintest idea who he was. And then he looked at me. He wasn't angry; he was reproachful. Disappointed. If I'm honest, that's worse. I was devastated. I couldn't believe I'd let Jesus down. I'd been so full of it. So full of good words and good intentions. But I couldn't back them up with my actions. I was so ashamed of myself, I ran out and wept. Wept like I've never wept before.

Friday was even worse. When Jesus needed his friends most, we deserted him – all of us, except John and some of the women in our group. It was fear that kept me away. What if they got me too and treated me the way they treated him? The one place I wanted to be was by Jesus' side – showing him that he could still depend on me and my support, yet I was too much of a coward.

So, I had to rely on others to keep me posted. And the news got worse and worse as the day wore on. First, they told me that he'd been put on trial for blasphemy, that the authorities wanted his blood; then, I heard about the beating, the insults, the scourging; and then they told me he'd been sentenced to death. Crucifixion. A death so horrible that Roman citizens are spared such awful treatment. Finally, I heard the news I thought I would never hear – he'd died.

Jesus. The miracle maker. My hero. My captain. My leader. The one who was going to save us all from oppression. Dead.

I was numb. Devastated. Didn't believe it. My hopes were snuffed out with him. What was I going to do now? Where would I go? Did you hear that I actually cut a man's ear off on Thursday night? One of the party who came to arrest Jesus. The man had it coming, if you asked me, but still, it wasn't a very clever thing to do. But Jesus healed him there and then. That's the kind of guy he was. That's why I couldn't believe that he'd died. You see, a man who could heal people in the blink of an eye. A man who could stop a storm. A man who could raise the dead. Well, that sort of man could save himself couldn't he? He couldn't be dead? So, why did he let them do that to him? Why did he let them kill him?

Saturday dragged on. I was exhausted, but couldn't sleep; hungry, but couldn't stomach anything. A small number of Jesus' followers gathered together in secret. We cried on each other's shoulders, basically. I found out from Mary Magdalene where he'd been buried. A man called Joseph of Arimathea gave up his tomb for Jesus' body to rest. I

*wanted to go there, to be with Jesus one last time, but it was the
Sabbath, so we couldn't go anywhere. I would have to wait until today
to pay my last respects to Jesus.*

*But then, this morning, something extraordinary happened. Mary
Magdalene came and told me that the stone blocking the entrance had
been rolled away. The tomb was empty. What? Empty? How was that
possible? She told me to go and see for myself. So that's what I did.*

*I ran to the tomb with John to check it out. To make sure that the
extreme emotion we'd all experienced hadn't got to Mary's head too
much. I could not believe it. She was right – the tomb was empty. I
went straight into the tomb and there were the grave clothes. But no
body. It had gone. Where was Jesus? Why was the tomb empty? Who
moved the stone?*

*Could the impossible have happened? Could Jesus be alive? I could
scarcely believe it. It was simply too good to be true. After all, dead
men don't rise from the dead. Do they?*

*Later, things got even more incredible! Mary told me that she'd met
with Jesus face to face – that she'd mistaken him for the gardener at
first, but then she knew it was him once he'd called her by name.
Perhaps it was true after all. Maybe Jesus was alive! Maybe he had
defeated death!*

*You're not going to believe the next thing that happened! I met
with him face to face! He appeared right in front of me. Out of
nowhere. It was really him. I could see the scars and everything. At
first, all the feelings of shame and guilt came flooding back. I couldn't
look him straight in the eye – how could I – I'd let him down so badly.
But then he spoke to me. He reassured me that he forgave me. That I
could start over again. He told me that I was still Rocky, that I still
had a part to play in the great adventure he's planned for me. In fact,
he told me that there were even more incredible days ahead. He said
that the adventure was only just beginning and that he would walk with
me and show me the way!*

*Suddenly I feel more excited than ever. I can't believe that so much
has happened in so little time. I can't wait to tell the other disciples that
I've seen Jesus and that he's alive! Back from the dead. God is truly at*

work in amazing ways. Jesus is alive! He has risen! I feel more alive than ever. If the adventure's only just begun, then bring it on!

- - - -

So, Peter met with Jesus and experienced a fresh sense of purpose and hope – and he was given the possibility of a brand new start. He discovered what it was to have his mistakes forgiven. Perhaps you need to know and experience God's forgiveness today. You can begin again. You too can have a fresh sense of purpose and hope. Jesus can give you that today.

But Jesus wasn't content to only give Peter that experience – he cared about the other disciples too. While the disciples were discussing excitedly the events on the road to Emmaus and Peter's life changing encounter, Jesus himself appeared among them, giving them the shock of their lives – they were terrified because they thought he was a ghost. The first thing he did is speak peace over them – "Peace be with you."

Then he reassured them that their eyes were not deceiving them. "I'm here, I'm real, I'm no ghost – look at my scars, you can touch me if you like."

Then, while they were still in a state of disbelief through joy and amazement, he asked them if they have any food to hand, and ate some fish in their presence. Ghosts don't do that either.

Then Jesus began to explain what it's all been about. He is risen – just as he promised he would be. He had told his disciples that he would be killed, but that he'd rise again on the third day. And why did this all have to happen in this way?

So repentance for the forgiveness of sins will be preached in his name to all nations, beginning at Jerusalem.

Jesus did all this to bring the possibility of a total life change for all people. We can know forgiveness and freedom from the things that bind us. When the world is so dreadfully troubled, we can know peace. When there is so much fear, we can know the presence of Jesus banishing that fear through his perfect, risen love. When death and illness is around us, Jesus brings hope. We can meet with him and know that hope for ourselves.

Finally, though at a time of crisis, Jesus also brings us purpose. He told his disciples …

> *"You are witnesses of these things. I am going to send you what my Father has promised; but stay in the city until you have been clothed with power from on high."*
> (vv.48-49)

He gives his disciples and he gives us a clear commission – all those things you've received from me – the peace, hope, forgiveness, love – I want you to tell others about this. I want you to be witnesses to me. Jesus has given us a job to do. And I believe that in these times, this world needs the good news of Jesus more than ever. Jesus has given us a job to do, to tell others about the lifechanging news of Jesus. He'll give us the power we need to do this job. Are we up for it?

PART 4
Easter
for
All Ages

A Brand New Start (John 20:1-18)

Dramatised Reading – John 20:1-18

Narrator: Early on the first day of the week, while it was still dark, Mary Magdalene went to the tomb and saw that the stone had been removed from the entrance. So she came running to Simon Peter and the other disciple, the one Jesus loved.

Mary: They have taken the Lord out of the tomb, and we don't know where they have put him!

Narrator: So Peter and the other disciple started for the tomb. Both were running, but the other disciple outran Peter and reached the tomb first. He bent over and looked in at the strips of linen lying there but did not go in. Then Simon Peter came along behind him and went straight into the tomb. He saw the strips of linen lying there, as well as the cloth that had been wrapped around Jesus' head. The cloth was still lying in its place, separate from the linen. Finally the other disciple, who had reached the tomb first, also went inside. He saw and believed. (They still did not understand from Scripture that Jesus had to rise from the dead.) Then the disciples went back to where they were staying.

Now Mary stood outside the tomb crying. As she wept, she bent over to look into the tomb and saw two angels in white, seated where Jesus' body had been, one at the head and the other at the foot.

Angels: Woman, why are you crying?

Mary: They have taken my Lord away, and I don't know where they have put him.

Narrator: At this, she turned around and saw Jesus standing there, but she did not realize that it was Jesus.

Jesus: Woman, why are you crying? Who is it you are looking for?

Mary: Sir, if you have carried him away, tell me where you have put him, and I will get him.

Jesus: Mary.

Mary: Rabboni!

Jesus: Do not hold on to me, for I have not yet ascended to the Father. Go instead to my brothers and tell them, 'I am ascending to my Father and your Father, to my God and your God.'

Narrator: Mary Magdalene went to the disciples with the news:

Mary: I have seen the Lord!

Narrator: And she told them what Jesus had said to her.

- - - -

Part 1 – Peter's Story

In 1 Corinthians 15, St Paul writes,

For what I received I passed on to you as of first importance: that Christ died for our sins according to the Scriptures, [4] that he was buried, that he was raised on the third day according to the Scriptures, [5] and that he appeared to Peter, and then to the Twelve.

Let's listen together to Peter's story:

I didn't sleep a wink. I couldn't. I felt so awful. Sick in the pit of my stomach. Those words he had said to me kept going round my head. "Tonight, before the cock crows, you'll deny you've ever known me." I couldn't believe it! Me, Peter, the one he'd nicknamed Rocky, deny Jesus? I'd never deny Jesus. Never. As if I could. He was the man who had given me purpose. Life was so exciting when he was around. I'd made lots of mistakes, but he forgave every one – amazing really. How could I ever deny the man who'd turned my life upside down? Who'd allowed me to share in the greatest adventure ever? I couldn't!

But I did. Three times. Swore I didn't have the faintest idea who he was. And then he looked at me. He wasn't angry; he was reproachful. Disappointed. If I'm honest, that's worse. I was devastated. I couldn't believe I'd let Jesus down. I'd been so full of it. So full of good words and good intentions. But I couldn't back them up with my actions. I was so ashamed of myself, I ran out and wept. Wept like I've never wept before.

Friday was even worse. When Jesus needed his friends most, we deserted him – all of us, except John and some of the women in our group. It was fear that kept me away. What if they got me too and treated me the way they treated him? The one place I wanted to be was by Jesus' side – showing him that he could still depend on me and my support, yet I was too much of a coward.

So I had to rely on others to keep me posted. And the news got worse and worse as the day wore on. First, they told me that he'd been put on trial for blasphemy, that the authorities wanted his blood; then, I heard about the beating, the insults, the scourging; and then they told me he'd been sentenced to death. Crucifixion. A death so horrible that Roman citizens are spared such awful treatment. Finally, I heard the news I thought I would never hear – he'd died.

Jesus. The miracle maker. My hero. My captain. My leader. The one who was going to save us all from oppression. Dead. I was numb. Devastated. Didn't believe it. My hopes were snuffed out with him. What was I going to do now? Where would I go?

Did you hear that I actually cut a man's ear off on Thursday night? One of the party who came to arrest Jesus. The man had it coming, if you asked me, but still, it wasn't a very clever thing to do. But Jesus healed him there and then. That's the kind of guy he was. That's why I couldn't believe that he'd died. You see, a man who could heal people in the blink of an eye. A man who could stop a storm. A man who could raise the dead. Well, that sort of man could save himself couldn't he? He couldn't be dead? So, why did he let them do that to him? Why did he let them kill him?

Saturday dragged on. I was exhausted, but couldn't sleep; hungry, but couldn't stomach anything. A small number of Jesus' followers gathered together in secret. We cried on each other's shoulders, basically. I found out from Mary Magdalene where he'd been buried. A man called Joseph of Arimathea gave up his tomb for Jesus' body to rest. I wanted to go there, to be with Jesus one last time, but it was the Sabbath, so we couldn't go anywhere. I would have to wait until today to pay my last respects to Jesus.

But then, this morning, something extraordinary happened. Mary Magdalene came and told me that the stone blocking the entrance had been rolled away. The tomb was empty. What? Empty? How was that possible? She told me to go and see for myself. So that's what I did.

I ran to the tomb with John to check it out. To make sure that the extreme emotion we'd all experienced hadn't got to Mary's head too much. I could not believe it. She was right – the tomb was empty. I went straight into the tomb and there were the grave clothes. But no body. It had gone. Where was Jesus? Why was the tomb empty? Who moved the stone? Could the impossible have happened? Could Jesus be alive? I could scarcely believe it. It was simply too good to be true. After all, dead men don't rise from the dead. Do they?

Later, things got even more incredible! Mary told me that she'd met with Jesus face to face – that she'd mistaken him for the gardener at first, but then she knew it was him once he'd called her by name. Perhaps it was true after all. Maybe Jesus was alive! Maybe he had defeated death!

You're not going to believe the next thing that happened! I met with him face to face! He appeared right in front of me. Out of nowhere. It was really him. I could see the scars and everything. At first, all the feelings of shame and guilt came flooding back. I couldn't look him straight in the eye – how could I – I'd let him down so badly. But then he spoke to me. He reassured me that he forgave me. That I could start over again. He told me that I was still Rocky, that I still had a part to play in the great adventure he's planned for me. In fact, he told me that there were even more incredible days ahead. He said that the adventure was only just beginning and that he would walk with me and show me the way!

Suddenly I feel more excited than ever. I can't believe that so much has happened in so little time. I can't wait to tell the other disciples that I've seen Jesus and that he's alive! Back from the dead. God is truly at work in amazing ways. Jesus is alive! He has risen! I feel more alive than ever. If the adventure's only just begun, then bring it on!

- - - -

Part 2 – Our Story

The tomb is empty. Jesus is alive. So what? If someone asked you today what relevance the death and resurrection of a man who lived 2,000 years ago still has, apart from being a wonderful story, how would you respond? What would you say? This is important stuff, and we need to think about how we'd respond to such a question. What does Jesus death and resurrection mean today? For you? For me?

If we look at the Bible and the lives of the disciples; the men and women who had been Jesus' companions and followers for three years before his awful death, we see something startling. Complete transformation. Take Peter. He was full of bold statements and good intentions, which proved to be hot air when it came to the crunch. He denied he'd ever known Jesus – three times! He must have been crushed afterwards. Guilty, and ashamed – a broken man. Some people may never recover from such an experience. However, the Bible records that within weeks he was the leader of this movement of people who claimed that Jesus had been raised from the dead. He was fearless in the face of questioning before the very religious leaders who'd conspired to have Jesus executed. He withstood imprisonment and persecution and refused to back down or change his story. You can read this all in the book of Acts. Finally, the testimony of the early church is that he was killed for his faith in the risen Lord Jesus.

What a transformation! Something must have happened to have brought about such a change in Peter. The only plausible explanation is that Jesus really did rise from the dead and that he really did know what it was to be forgiven and restored, empowered to make a brand new start.

We, like Peter, can know that for ourselves. There have been times when I have felt so unworthy, so dirty, so bogged down in my sinfulness and shame, that I've been unable to believe that God could possibly be prepared to forgive me for the awful things I've done, let alone to restore me and empower me in his work. But the beautiful, crazy truth of the Gospel is that no matter how bad, inadequate or hopeless you feel, God has his arms wide open, ready to forgive and restore you. He has a plan and a purpose for you. Peter learned that then and many of us have learned that now. The first meaning of the resurrection for us today, then, is that we can know what it is to be forgiven and restored.

The second meaning of the resurrection is that we can know what it is to no longer be afraid anymore. Peter saw that

Jesus was alive and knew that death no longer had any power over him. If Jesus could be raised from the dead, then Peter could too. As St. Paul writes in 1 Corinthians, "Now Christ has been raised from the dead, … In Christ all will be made alive." (1 Cor 15:20,22). The worst thing that any one can ever do to you is to kill you. But thanks to Jesus, there is the hope of new life at the other side. That's why Peter was able to be fearless in the face of persecution and imprisonment – he had put his trust in one who was far more powerful than the most powerful of dictators. Death simply has no power any more. Because Jesus has overcome the grave.

And that's as true for us today as it was for Peter then. We need not fear death, because Jesus has gone there before us and come out the other side. Through his power we will rise from the dead. This means that no matter what the world throws at us, we can, in God's power, overcome it. We don't need to be afraid anymore, because the tomb is empty and death has been defeated.

Finally, the third meaning of the resurrection is that Jesus' work continues. His was a life characterised by radical love, compassion, and transformation. His disciples continued that work – healing the sick, proclaiming God's indiscriminate love, and beginning a revolution that's still not finished. And the baton's been passed to us. Not far from these doors there are lost people who need to be found, broken people who need to encounter the healing love of Jesus, people who need to discover hope and purpose, that can only be found in Jesus. Jesus is alive. He invites us to join the revolution, to be history makers. We cannot do it on our own, but we have his resurrection blood coursing through our veins, and because of that, nothing is impossible. Are we up for it?

The Breath of New Life (John 20:1-18)

Narnia Sketch – Part 1

Narrator: I want you to come with me to Narnia. A world that's ruled by the White Witch.

[WITCH comes onto stage]

Narrator: A world where it's always Winter and never Christmas, and certainly, never Spring.

[CHILDREN   come onto stage, dressed in Winter Clothes and play/skip, etc.]

Narrator: Always winter, never Christmas. This is like the effect of evil in our world. It affects everybody in some way or another. The world's not as nice as it should be. There are places where people are fighting and killing each other. There are places where many are sick. There are places where people die because they don't have enough food   Closer to home, if we're honest, our families, our schools, our church – they're not as nice as they should be.
                   And in Narnia, they know that they cannot defeat the witch. They cannot make the spring come. They need a rescuer – they hear that Aslan the Lion is on his way.

Children: If we trust Aslan, he'll sort it out.

Narrator: Unfortunately, the witch also hears that Aslan's on his way, and she's not at all happy about it.

Witch:	Aslan's coming? Not if I can help it. I must stop him. – I know, I'll get Edmund to help me. [To Edmund, who stands apart from the rest] Edmund, you look lonely. I'll look after you – could you tell me where Aslan is?
Edmund:	He's over there.
Narrator:	So Edmund betrays Aslan. And even worse, the Witch comes near and turns people into statues

[WITCH walks past some children and they stand still.]

Children:	Oh no! We can't get ourselves out of this mess.
Narrator:	They're right, you know, they can't solve the mess. Only Aslan could do that for them. As for Edmund. He's in big trouble. He has to pay for betraying Aslan, and the price he has to pay is death. But Aslan comes.
Aslan:	White Witch, I will take Edmund's place. I will give up my life for him.
Witch:	That's fine by me. Then die!

[ASLAN lies on the ground.]

Narrator:	Aslan has done nothing wrong, and yet he agrees to take Edmund's place. He gives up his life for Edmund. Dies in his place. Right everybody, sit down where you are … we'll come back to Narnia in a minute.

The story of our world is that we all bring trouble on ourselves sometimes, and we can't always fix it on our own. This was how the world found itself on Good Friday. We were in a mess, and had no ability to fix things. We needed a Saviour. Jesus was that Saviour. Though he'd done nothing wrong, he gave up his life in our place. And on Good Friday, when Jesus died, the world seemed in even more of a mess, because an innocent man died. Jesus' friends were devastated.

Meanwhile, in Narnia. Susan and Lucy saw Aslan die. They stayed by his body and wept. Let's find out what happens next.

[At this point play clip from Chronicles of Narnia: The Lion, the Witch and the Wardrobe – "Aslan rises again"

Narnia Sketch – Part 2

Narrator: Can I have you back in your frozen positions, everyone? Aslan has come back to life. – Aslan, can you stand up? By offering himself in the place of Edmund, he has broken the curse – in his words, death itself has rolled back. The everlasting winter comes to an end – spring comes. Aslan defeats the witch and breathes life into the people who have been turned into statues.

[ASLAN walks around and breathes on the children who start to move around and play again.]

Gospel Reading – Matthew 28:1-10

[1] After the Sabbath, at dawn on the first day of the week, Mary Magdalene and the other Mary went to look at the tomb.
[2] There was a violent earthquake, for an angel of the Lord came down from heaven and, going to the tomb, rolled back the stone and sat on it.
[3] His appearance was like lightning, and his clothes were white as snow.

⁴ The guards were so afraid of him that they shook and became like dead men.
⁵ The angel said to the women, 'Do not be afraid, for I know that you are looking for Jesus, who was crucified. ⁶ He is not here; he has risen, just as he said. Come and see the place where he lay. ⁷ Then go quickly and tell his disciples: "He has risen from the dead and is going ahead of you into Galilee. There you will see him." Now I have told you.'
⁸ So the women hurried away from the tomb, afraid yet filled with joy, and ran to tell his disciples. ⁹ Suddenly Jesus met them. 'Greetings,' he said. They came to him, clasped his feet and worshipped him. ¹⁰ Then Jesus said to them, 'Do not be afraid. Go and tell my brothers to go to Galilee; there they will see me.'

Summary

When C.S. Lewis wrote *The Lion, the Witch and the Wardrobe*, he clearly meant for us to see parallels between Aslan and Jesus, between the moment Aslan willingly lays down his life to save Edmund the betrayer, and the way that Jesus willingly went to the cross. Jesus had done nothing wrong. He was innocent, and he took our place. When Good Friday was over, it seemed like a tragedy. It was the saddest day. Like Lucy and Susan in *the Lion, the Witch and the Wardrobe,* Jesus' friends had watched him die. They were so sad. There would have been many tears. They wanted to go to the tomb to be close to him somehow, so they went as soon as they could, early on Sunday morning. But Jesus' body wasn't in the tomb. They met an angel, who told them something amazing …

> *"Do not be afraid, for I know that you are looking for Jesus, who was crucified. He is not here; he has risen, just as he said. Come and see the place where he lay."*
(vv.5-6).

They looked, and incredibly, the angel was right – the tomb was empty. Jesus had gone. But then, something even more amazing happened …

So the women hurried away from the tomb, afraid yet filled with joy, and ran to tell his disciples. Suddenly Jesus met them. 'Greetings,' he said. They came to him, clasped his feet and worshipped him. Then Jesus said to them, 'Do not be afraid. Go and tell my brothers to go to Galilee; there they will see me.'
(vv.8-10)

They met Jesus himself face to face. Imagine the joy they must have felt! It changed everything. Suddenly, what looked like the greatest defeat was actually the greatest victory. In dying, Jesus took on all of our sin, he stepped in our place. He took on death itself. By rising again, Jesus broke the curse of sin. Death itself has been defeated. This is the story of easter. This is what we've gathered today to celebrate.

Without Jesus all we would have to look forward to would be an everlasting winter of sadness, sickness and an eternity of darkness. The world is blighted by the dark magic of evil that brings death and suffering. But Jesus came so we could experience spring. He came to bring new hope and breathe new life to the world. At Easter, a deeper magic brought Jesus back to life and now Jesus Christ brings life to the whole world. He saves us when we've messed up and he brings life and meaning to every day.

Sometimes we act as if we're frozen, and we think that God isn't powerful enough to bring summer in our lives. Maybe our problems are too big. The empty tomb tells us that there is no problem that is too big for Jesus to help us with. The tomb is empty. He is alive. There's a wonderful moment in the Gospels after he's risen again, when Jesus breathes on the disciples, and says to them, receive the Holy Spirit. He breathes life into them and it brings about huge transformation for them. We're here today, because of that transformation, because they went from being in hiding, to fearlessly proclaiming that Jesus is risen. Jesus says to us too, I can bring that transformation in your life, if you'll let me. Will we do that, will we let Jesus breathe new life into us?

Some of us might see the Easter story as just a nice story, like Narnia. But what if it's more than that? What if the tomb is really empty? What if he really has taken away our sin and given us new life?

In the Bible, A man named Nicodemus went to Jesus and asked him how to get to heaven. Nicodemus was probably a better person than any of us. He was a leader of Israel, a man who studied the scriptures, quoted the scriptures, sang the scriptures. He obeyed all the laws of God. You would have expected Jesus to pat him on the back and say "Well done. Heaven is waiting for you." But he doesn't. Jesus says, "You must be born again." And that means to give God all of your heart and all of your life. Some of us might want to do that today. If you would like to, then please join with me in praying the following prayer …

Dear Lord Jesus,
Thank you that you died on the cross in my place so that I could be forgiven.
Thank you that you rose again to bring new life and new hope to the world.
Would you come in my heart and breathe new life in me.
Help me to follow you every day of my life.
Amen.

The Day Everything Changed (John 20:1-18)

This was an all-age talk where we interspersed a monologue with more conventional teaching. Have someone playing the part of Mary Magdalene and someone different being the other voice.

I made my way numbly to the tomb that Sunday morning. I hadn't slept a wink since Friday, when my world fell apart, when I saw my Lord being laid to rest in that cold, dark tomb. I spent most of the time since then weeping. That man, my Rabbi, wasn't just any other man; he was the one on whom I had pinned my hopes. And I watched him die. It was so awful.

Before he came along, I was nothing – an outcast, plagued by seven demons; evil spirits that raged inside me – voices I neither recognised nor wanted to recognise. They wouldn't leave me alone. And then Jesus released me; he allowed me to hope again. So I followed him and witnessed incredible things. As well as that amazing teaching he performed incredible miracles: he healed the sick, cast out demons and even raised the dead. Amazing. Surely this man was the Messiah – the promised king who would rescue the Jewish people from all of their oppressors. As time passed, my hopes grew – my hopes and all of the others too. Only last week he entered Jerusalem riding on a donkey as the crowds shouted, "Hosanna to the Son of David! Blessed is he who comes in the name of the Lord!"

The excitement grew … and then … and then … I could scarcely believe it … it all went horribly wrong. The reports came on Friday morning that he had been arrested and the next thing I knew I was watching him die. Crucifixion was an awful thing, but it was even worse when the man being crucified was the man you'd loved and on whom you'd pinned all your hopes. People mocked him, saying that he should save himself if he were the Son of God – and I hoped that he'd do just that – after all, I knew he had the power to. And I continued hoping, but that hope got smaller and smaller the shallower his breathing got. And then finally, he breathed his last with a final cry, "It is finished" and my hope had gone. I was devastated. It was all over.

The rest of that day are a blur really. Me and the other Marys, and Salome, who'd been with him when he was dying, we began to wonder what would happen to Jesus now. Who would look after him? Thankfully a kind man, Joseph of Arimathea said he would ensure Jesus was laid in his own family tomb. He arranged for Jesus' body to be taken down from the cross, and took it to the grave. We followed; we wanted to know where they would lay him, so we could pay our last respects and care for him. We went back to our lodgings in the city and got spices and ointment ready to anoint his body. But the Sabbath was just starting, so we had to rest. It was so hard. We were reeling from all that had happened, all that we had lost.

Early on the Sunday morning, we went to the tomb. This was our chance to serve Jesus one last time, by giving the body the care it deserved. But the stone had been moved – Jesus body was no longer there! As if Jesus hadn't undergone enough already, now his body had been stolen. It added insult to awful injury. I ran to tell Simon Peter and the disciple Jesus loved, saying, "They have taken the Lord out of the tomb, and we don't know where they have put him!"

Impulsive Peter and the other disciple didn't believe me, of course, and ran off to check out my story. I was left behind. In bits. Now I was weeping, not simply because Jesus was dead, but because they'd stolen his body. The one thing that had been left to me – the simple act of giving his body the treatment he deserved – even that had been taken away from me. My head was spinning. I didn't know what else to do, so

I went back to the tomb, stumbling there through the tears. Why? Because I probably didn't have anywhere else to go. I felt that by being at the tomb, I would somehow feel closer to Jesus.

But then, something very unexpected happened. I was standing outside the tomb, weeping. I bent over to look into the tomb, double checking I wasn't imagining it all, and there were two angels in white there, seated where Jesus' body had been, one at the head and the other at the foot. They asked me why I was crying, so I told them, "They have taken my Lord away and I don't know where they have put him."

I don't think I was really comprehending I was talking with angels – not your everyday occurrence, is it? All I could think about was the fact my Lord's body had gone. It was all too much – shock, grief, bewilderment – were all swirling round my mind.

- - - -

Let's pause there and rest in the sense of bewilderment, shock and despair. Because we know the end of the story, we gloss over the devastation that probably swept over Mary. But I think that to do so is to a mistake. There is a myth that Christian experience is all hunky dory; that once we come to faith in Jesus, everything will be easy and that we will always be joyful.

We expect that every day will be like Easter, but then awful things happen. Someone we love falls ill and then, despite our fervent prayers, they die. We experience the bitterness of divorce; our children deny the faith that is at the centre of our very beings. Whatever it is, we feel something like Mary did – hurting, lost, despairing and angry. It seems like too many days are like that awful Friday, or like that moment we've just paused on that Easter morning before the penny drops.

This morning I feel that I have to say one thing – that experience of brokenness and despair that you are going through; it's ok to feel like that. Just dip in the Psalms and you'll see that there is a lot of anger and despair around. You're not abnormal. If you want to shout at God, then that's ok – if you find yourself constantly asking "WHY", that's ok too – God knows. I'll say that again – he knows.

But that needn't be the end of the end of the story. God doesn't want to leave you like that. Mary Magdalene was in the depths of despair, but that changed.

Let's re-join the story, to see how ...

- - - -

Suddenly I saw someone in the corner of my eye – perhaps he could help. I didn't know who he was, I couldn't see properly, my eyes were so blurred by tears.

He asked me, "Woman, why are you crying? Who is it you are looking for?"

I thought he was the gardener; I wasn't sure who else would be hanging around. Perhaps he had something to do with the disappearance of Jesus' body? "Sir, if you have carried him away, tell me where you have put him, and I will get him."

- - - -

Let's pause there again. The first thing Jesus does is to ask Mary why she's crying. Of course, he knows already, but he wants her to tell him, for her to allow him to help.

And I believe that today, he is asking us the same question. If there is something troubling you, that causes you an ache in your heart, Jesus knows it already, but he longs for you to share it with him. Why are you crying? Why are you hurting?

Let's just be quiet for a moment and name that in our hearts – because Jesus wants to share our burdens, to listen to our pain.

Let's go back to the passage again. Mary thinks that Jesus is the gardener, so she asks him if he'd moved the body and if so, where it was.

Even though he's standing there in front of her, Mary's grief blinds her to his true identity.

- - - -

Everything changed with one word. "Mary." The penny finally dropped. It dawned on me who this man was – that the man who'd set me free from those demons, who'd taught incredible things and done wonderful works and who I'd watched die just two days previously; this was the man who wonderfully, incredibly, but truly, was alive. I couldn't believe it. All I wanted to do was hold on to him and never let go, to stay in this moment, hoping it would never end.

Jesus extracted himself from me with a smile. "Mary, don't cling on to me. I need you to go and tell my disciples. Tell them that I've risen from the grave, just as I said I would. So, I tore myself away from Jesus, then rushed off back to Jesus' disciples, with this most incredible news, "I have seen the Lord!"

- - - -

Jesus is alive. And that is why we can hope again. He wants us to tell him why we're hurting, he wants to share our burdens.

He calls us by name, because he wants us to see and to grow to understand who he really is. He is the risen Lord Jesus, who experienced the most incredible suffering that none of us will ever fully understand, but then he overcame the greatest enemies, sin and death. He is the reason we can hope.

He is Jesus, who is God in human form, who loved the world so much that he lived a fully human life, experiencing every emotion and experience, who died on the cross, but amazingly rose from the dead, showing us that he is king over sin, suffering and death – that he has overcome them all, and that he is Lord of life.

It is the same Jesus who knows us each by name, who knows everything we are going through and wants to meet us in the midst of our suffering and set us free. He is with us in our darkest hour and can bring us strength, comfort, peace and hope – hope that the pain and sorrow will end forever, and be replaced by unending and unfailing joy and peace.

This is Jesus, who restores us and brings hope out of despair.

If you don't yet have this life-changing, hope-filling relationship with Jesus, Easter is a great time to begin or renew this transforming relationship. Speak to me afterwards if you want to know more.

This is Jesus. He is risen. He is alive. Alleluia!

- - - -

Prayers – Responding to God

Give each person a stone or pebble, or a stone shape cut-out of paper. Ask people to look at their stone as they think of a situation which seems hopeless.

Give one or two examples, such as a friendship which has gone wrong, a country where there is war or something that is affecting your particular gathering of Christians.

As a resurrection song is played quietly (for example, Forever by Bethel Music), invite the congregation to bring the stones forward to lay at a focal point – an Easter garden, or the foot of a cross, maybe – as a sign of God's desire to roll away our stones of hopelessness and replace them with new beginnings.

If you wish, you could lead into a brief time of Intercession, using the following responses between prayers for the world, your locality and individual situations.

Where hope seems buried…

Resurrected Lord, bring new life

The Foolishness of Easter

This service was based around the fact that Easter Sunday happened to coincide with April Fool's Day and was inspired in part by a blog I wrote about the fact that the Gospel seems like foolishness.[*]

Introduction: Best April Fools' Adverts

Here are some of the best April Fools' Adverts in recent years …

1) Tesco … Shoppers will soon have their weekly shop taken to a whole new level of fun as Tesco takes a leap forward in revolutionising the shopping experience with the introduction of trampoline inspired bouncy aisles, which will help people reach the top shelves more easily.

2) The Royal National Institute for the Blind are recruiting an army of cats for its new CATNAV scheme...... Sight loss charity RNIB's new scheme CATNAV is to train thousands of cats to act as mobility guides for blind and partially sighted people.

3) Leading the way in taxi innovation, cab app Hailo today launches its brand new feature to help city dwellers get around more easily. Using Hailo's new Piggyback function from their smartphone, users will see one of Hailo's specially trained human piggyback carriers arrive in a matter of minutes to transport the passenger to their

---

[*] Ian Paul, "What sort of fool is this Jesus", *Psephizo*, https://www.psephizo.com/biblical-studies/what-sort-of-fool-is-this-jesus/

destination. With the ability to dart in between traffic, Hailo's Piggybackers have been recruited for their athleticism and knowledge of the city, as well as allowing passengers to enjoy a 360 degree view of their surroundings.

4) Tweets sent by Greater Manchester Police which sparked a dead of night Twitter alert after urging followers to vote for their "favourite" prison inmate to get them freed early as part of an April Fools prank. Officers in Radcliffe, Greater Manchester used the force Twitter page to post a midnight message on the site stating: "Know someone in prison? You can get them released early by voting for them on here. The prisoners with the most votes also wins a holiday."

5) 'Marmite Clear' is here... The makers of the nation's favourite savoury spread have today announced the launch of an innovative new product ' Marmite Clear'. Leading the way in spreadable innovation, the brand is evolving its iconic brown shade to create an all new translucent version of the classic British breakfast condiment.

Today we celebrate Easter Sunday. The day when we proclaim that a dead man rose again. People call this foolish, just a story. But this morning, we'll be discovering how this one day changed everything.

- - - -

Quiz: April Fool or April Fact

We're going to have an April Fool quiz – can you work out which of these are April Fools or April Fact?

1) There is a small country in the Atlantic called San Serriffe, made up of a number of islands in the shape of a semi-colon.

April Fool - The Guardian ran a seven-page supplement in the style of other reviews of foreign countries that it often ran. Most of San Serriffe's place names and characters were puns and plays on words relating to printing.

2) A television programme called 'Dogs Might Fly' saw canines being trained to fly planes.

April Fact - This was a real series aired on Sky 1.

3) In 1976, Pluto passed behind Jupiter, causing a gravitational alignment that briefly reduced the Earth's own gravity.

April Fool - Patrick Moore announced the hoax during an interview on Radio 2. Many people claimed to feel the shift in gravity.

4) A Burger King fanatic changed his name to Bacon Double Cheeseburger by deed poll. –

April Fact - Formerly Simon Smith, the 33-year-old man decided he fancied a change and his usual Burger King order was the first thing that popped his head.

5) North Korean despot Kim Jong Un banned One Direction from entering the country unless they get their hair cut.

April Fool - This was a hoax from the Mirror in 2014.

- - - -

<u>Quiz: Easter Fool or Easter Fact</u>

Now we're going to test you on your knowledge of the Easter story from the Bible – is it Easter Fact or Easter Fool?

1) Judas betrayed Jesus to the Jewish High Priests for 30 pieces of gold.

<u>Easter Fool</u> – 30 pieces of silver

2) Jesus prayed that He would not have to suffer.

<u>Easter Fact</u> – in Garden of Gethsemane

3) The crowds tried to persuade the Jewish Leaders to crucify Jesus.

<u>Easter Fool</u> – it was the other way round. The Jewish leaders stirred up the crowd. Jesus was incredibly popular with the people, which is why he was arrested at night.

4) Peter, Jesus' closest disciple, denied ever knowing him.

<u>Easter Fact</u> – despite swearing adamantly that he would never deny Jesus.

5) Most of Jesus' disciples were all there when he was dying on the cross.

<u>Easter Fool</u> – most had fled. Only John and some of the women were there at the cross when Jesus died.

6) The disciples did not believe Jesus would die and be resurrected.

Easter Fact – they certainly weren't waiting for him to rise from the dead that Sunday morning. This is despite Jesus having told them this would all happen a number of times.

7) The tomb was left unattended after Jesus had been buried.

Easter Fool – because Jesus had claimed he would rise from the dead, the Jewish leaders had some guards posted at the tomb's entrance to ensure that the disciples wouldn't be able to steal his body and falsely claim he'd risen.

8) The first to hear of the Risen Christ were Peter and John.

Easter Fool – it was Mary, Mary Magdalene and Salome. Mary Magdalene was the first to encounter Jesus and the first person entrusted with the news he was alive.

9) A rumour was started that the disciples stole Jesus' body.

Easter Fact – when the guards who'd been protecting the tomb came back to the authorities and told them what had happened, they were bribed so that they would spread this false rumour about the disciples.

10) The risen Jesus appeared only to the disciples.

Easter Fool – actually, there were a number of resurrection appearances recorded in the Gospels over a 40 day period to a number of different people. St Paul also refers to 150 people seeing the risen Jesus at once.

- - - -

Talk – Part 1

This was delivered as if by a court jester, wearing a jester's hat.

I want to tell you the real story
of Jesus the king and his crazy glory.
He broke all the rules, didn't play by the book
Want to know why? well let's take a look
Begin at the beginning, with his birth
Circumstances of which were quite absurd.
If you were a king you'd be born to a queen
In a castle or palace, you know what I mean!

This king was born and placed in a manger
Where, if you ask me, he was in danger
Of being eaten by animals or at least licked
Not the birth place I'd have picked.
As for his mother she was dirt poor
and came from Nazareth (somewhere obscure).
The father was God - or that's what they said,
(Though sceptics scoffed and blamed Joseph instead).

And the first ones to visit this family
Were men who had sheep for company,
then wise men from distant lands afar
lined up to pay homage - they'd followed the star.
It was all a bit weird, no nobles in sight,
Not the normal guests that kings would invite.
All in all, so far and so strange,
Can you believe God this would arrange?

Then what we get is three decades of silence;
When he could use the time to form an alliance
Of powerful people to back up his claim,
Paving the way for power and fame.
Instead he settled for obscurity:
A lifetime of learning, obeying Mary.
He took up his tools, and learned his dad's trade
Until God gave the nod - it was God's game he played.

When the time came to step into the light,
He still didn't seem to get anything right.
He stayed in the North, far from centres of power,
Said something about it not being his hour.
He spent all his time with all the wrong folk -
to outcasts and poor, the good news he spoke.
The good news he spread through great acts of healing;
he even touched lepers, now that's not appealing.

The people they loved him - well, most of them did.
Others were jealous and planned to get rid
of this rabbi who simply made them look bad
and threatened their power (what power they had).
But he wasn't afraid of the powerful folks;
Instead they became the butt of his jokes.
As you imagine this didn't go down
well with the ones who were close to the crown.

In Jerusalem (the capital city)
the leaders formed a deathly committee.
Dark deeds were plotted, they formed a plan
That would end the life of the miracle man.
So, they waited and watched, bided their time
for the perfect moment to commit their crime.
And soon that time came - the Great Festival.
This man would be silenced once and for all.

This King knew their plans, saw into their hearts
Could have stayed where he was, didn't need to depart.
But obedient to God, he made his way down
to Jerusalem (that is, David's old town).
There crowds greeted him, hailed him as King
Lining the streets to cheer and to sing
songs of joy and of hope - a new day was dawning.
By the end of the week, they'd all be mourning.

It went downhill so fast, the vengeance was swift
Jesus' friend Judas gave them a gift
- in exchange for some money - he'd show them where
to capture Jesus, when no-one was there.
So, dead of night, they came armed to the teeth
to arrest this King, this prince of peace.
As for his friends - well, most of them fled,
Left him alone to face the trial ahead.

The rulers now had him right where they wanted
they beat him and tortured, his words they distorted.
They lied and colluded, schemed and connived,
He wouldn't be leaving this city alive.
He was sentenced to death and nailed to a cross.
The rulers had triumphed, showed who was boss.
"This King, what a fool!" they sneered and said,
"His dream is over, it's finished, he's dead."

And is that the end of this King's story?
Has it really finished, with death, not with glory?

- - - -

Gospel Reading —Mark 16:1-8

When the Sabbath was over, Mary Magdalene, Mary the mother of James, and Salome bought spices so that they might go to anoint Jesus' body. Very early on the first day of the week, just after sunrise, they were on their way to the tomb and they asked each other, 'Who will roll the stone away from the entrance of the tomb?'

But when they looked up, they saw that the stone, which was very large, had been rolled away. As they entered the tomb, they saw a young man dressed in a white robe sitting on the right side, and they were alarmed.

'Don't be alarmed,' he said. 'You are looking for Jesus the Nazarene, who was crucified. He has risen! He is not here. See the place where they laid him. But go, tell his disciples and Peter, "He is going ahead of you into Galilee. There you will see him, just as he told you."'

Trembling and bewildered, the women went out and fled from the tomb. They said nothing to anyone, because they were afraid.

- - - -

Illustration: Disappearing Bunny trick

As a bit of fun, we made a chocolate bunny "disappear". Buy 3 chocolate bunnies. Prepare one of them in advance, by removing it from the wrapping and very carefully reshaping the wrapping so it looks as though there is a chocolate bunny still in it. Line the three up next to each other. Making one "disappear" by getting people to look in a different direction, before knocking it off the table, make the

other "disappear" by eating it. Then, after a dramatic build
up, flatten the third bunny in a swift and loud movement.
You've made it disappear!

- - - -

Talk – Part 2

So far and so bad, the King is now dead.
Laid in the tomb, when all friends had fled.
They must have felt foolish to trust in this man,
To have dared to dream, to follow his plan.
Grief-stricken and stunned, they all hide away
Until early in the morning one special Sunday
Two Marys and Salome head to the grave
Find the stone rolled away from the front of the cave.

Jesus' body's gone – there's an angel instead
Tells the disbelieving women he's alive, he's not dead.
"He is risen, as he told you, this is how it had to be."
Then Mary turns round, and through tears she can see
The risen Lord Jesus who calls her by name –
"Mary" – "Rabboni", on her knees she exclaims.
Then he sends her to tell Peter and all Jesus' friends
That this story's not over, this is not where it ends.

And it doesn't stop there, no it just carries on
as the disciples pick up their Saviour's baton
They give all they have to tell people the news
Of this crazy King's love for Gentiles and Jews.
He died, but he's risen. There is hope for mankind,
Through the deepest of darkness a new light will shine.
Hatred and death your day is now done
For hope, love and life the victory have won.

And this foolish King looks to me and to you
invites us to be part of this story too.
Will we, with his flame burning inside
Tell others of grace and hope that's alive.
Will we be fools for Christ, he invites us to choose
To give up our rights - we've nothing to lose -
Because we'll gain life in all of its glory
Taking our place in his everlasting story.

Through his words and his deeds his message rings through
that God's love is boundless for me and for you
Wherever we've strayed, whatever we've done,
there's always a way back to the arms of the Son.
Thanks to the events of that Sunday morning
There'll always be hope that a new day is dawning.
So, come let us celebrate Jesus the King
and hope that he makes us as foolish as him.

PART 5
Responding
to Hope

The Passion Ballad

All eyes on a garden - a kneeling man
Cries out to his father, "Take this cup if you can."
A gasp heard in heaven - angels can't bear
Watch the scene of a broken man crying down there.

The fate of the world is now left unsure,
The plan for salvation could stutter and fall.
It hangs on a man who feels so much pain;
His burden is great, his sweat falls like rain.

Urgent discussion - is there a way out?
No sign of the Father, beginnings of doubt.
Fervently pray that the man will find strength,
Agonised moment, unspeakable length.

Until . . .

A look of decision. All heaven awaits.
Resolution is formed, no time for debate.
"Not my will but yours," he'll follow the way
Ordained by the Father. He'll face the next day.

All happens so quickly - soldiers arrive.
Fulfil their destiny, keep our hope alive.
Man stands on trial; he's committed no wrong.
Agony in heaven as the Father looks on.

A sprinkle of water - case is dismissed
In the hands of the Jews who betrayed with a kiss.
The sentence is passed: a criminal's death.
Hang on a cross, no dignity left.

Each blow of nails through hands and through feet
Echoes through heaven - a desperate beat.
The Father winces as his son hangs down there
In desolate loneliness, there's no one to care.

Dignitaries mock as the sinless one dies.
"Father, forgive," is all he replies.
His life ebbs away, the darkness descends.
"It is finished!" he shouts. The struggle just ends.

Leaderless people - the light has gone out.
Fail to see what the anguish was about.
They don't understand that he had to die;
They secretly mourn, and simply ask why.

The third day dawns and it all becomes clear:
The tomb is empty, there's nobody here.
"The Lord is alive," the angels rejoice.
Relief in heaven, for he made the right choice.

The great gamble worked - he carried our sin,
Died on the cross so we could go in.
United to the Father through the Son.
Mission accomplished and the victory won.

<u>One Saturday</u>

A headline in the paper read,
"Religious nut and freak is dead."
The spokesman for the Pharisees
Explained (while looking very pleased),
"This man had caused us lots of trouble,
We had to get him on the double.
He claimed he was the Chosen One,
Almighty God, His only Son.
We Pharisees weren't having that! –
Even worse, he claimed he'd sat
At God's right hand in heaven above
And will again. You know, I'd love
To see that day, but won't of course –
For that man's words are just a source
Of claptrap and of blasphemy,
That's why we killed him, can't you see?
He drew the crowds with clever tricks –
They even claimed he'd healed the sick.
The blind can see (or so they claim)
And crippled people walk again!
But that's not all – you'll laugh at this –
A *dead* man (said with emphasis)
Was brought back to life at his word –
This claim's preposterous, quite absurd.
We all know that dead men don't walk
About, or eat and drink and talk.
It's clear to me they've all been had.
Poor, simple people fooled – how sad!
At first we'd tried to humour him
Until he got beneath our skin.
He insulted us, called us snakes,
Told us that we were on the make.

We couldn't take it any more,
That really was the final straw.
We had him silenced, put to death,
This carpenter from Nazareth.
Let's see him speak against us now –
As he's dead, I can't see how!
He could rise again and death defy."
The spokesman spat, "And pigs might fly!"

Jesus the King and his Crazy Glory

Part 1

I want to tell you the real story
of Jesus the king and his crazy glory.
He broke all the rules, didn't play by the book
Want to know why? well let's take a look!
Begin at the beginning, with his birth
Circumstances of which were quite absurd.
If you were a king you'd be born to a queen
In a castle or palace, you know what I mean!

This king was born and placed in a manger
Where, if you ask me, he was in danger
Of being eaten by animals or at least licked
Not the birth place I'd have picked.
As for his mother she was dirt poor
and came from Nazareth (somewhere obscure).
The father was God - or that's what they said,
(Though sceptics scoffed and blamed Joseph instead).

And the first ones to visit this family
Were men who had sheep for company,
then wise men from distant lands afar
lined up to pay homage - they'd followed the star.
It was all a bit weird, no nobles in sight,
Not the normal guests that kings would invite.
All in all, so far and so strange,
Can you believe God this would arrange?

Then what we get is three decades of silence;
When he could use the time to form an alliance
Of powerful people to back up his claim,
Paving the way for power and fame.
Instead, he settled for obscurity:
A lifetime of learning, obeying Mary.
He took up his tools, and learned his dad's trade
Until God gave the nod - it was God's game he played.

When the time came to step into the light,
He still didn't seem to get anything right.
He stayed in the North, far from centres of power,
Said something about it not being his hour.
He spent all his time with all the wrong folk -
to outcasts and poor, the good news he spoke.
The good news he spread through great acts of healing;
he even touched lepers, now that's not appealing.

The people they loved him - well, most of them did.
Others were jealous and planned to get rid
of this rabbi who simply made them look bad
and threatened their power (what power they had).
But he wasn't afraid of the powerful folks;
Instead they became the butt of his jokes.
As you imagine this didn't go down
well with the ones who were close to the crown.

In Jerusalem (the capital city)
the leaders formed a deathly committee.
Dark deeds were plotted, they formed a plan
That would end the life of the miracle man.
So, they waited and watched, bided their time
for the perfect moment to commit their crime.
And soon that time came - the Great Festival.
This man would be silenced once and for all.

This King knew their plans, saw into their hearts
Could have stayed where he was, didn't need to depart.
But obedient to God, he made his way down
to Jerusalem (that is, David's old town).
There crowds greeted him, hailed him as King
Lining the streets to cheer and to sing
songs of joy and of hope - a new day was dawning.
By the end of the week, they'd all be mourning.

It went downhill so fast, the vengeance was swift
Jesus' friend Judas gave them a gift
- in exchange for some money - he'd show them where
to capture Jesus when no-one was there.
So, dead of night, they came armed to the teeth
to arrest this King, this prince of peace.
As for his friends - well, most of them fled,
Left him alone to face the trial ahead.

The rulers now had him right where they wanted
they beat him and tortured, his words they distorted.
They lied and colluded, schemed and connived,
He wouldn't be leaving this city alive.
He was sentenced to death and nailed to a cross.
The rulers had triumphed, showed who was boss.
"This King, what a fool!" they sneered and said,
"His dream is over, it's finished, he's dead."

And is that the end of this King's story?
Has it really finished, with death, not with glory?

Part 2

So far and so bad, the King is now dead.
Laid in the tomb, when all friends had fled.
They must have felt foolish to trust in this man,
To have dared to dream, to follow his plan.
Grief-stricken and stunned, they all hide away
Until early in the morning one special Sunday
Two Marys and Salome head to the grave
Find the stone rolled away from the front of the cave.

Jesus' body's gone – there's an angel instead
Tells the disbelieving women he's alive, he's not dead.
"He is risen, as he told you, this is how it had to be."
Then Mary turns round, and through tears she can see
The risen Lord Jesus who calls her by name –
"Mary" – "Rabboni", on her knees she exclaims.
Then he sends her to tell Peter and all Jesus' friends
That this story's not over, this is not where it ends.

And it doesn't stop there, no it just carries on
as the disciples pick up their Saviour's baton
They give all they have to tell people the news
Of this crazy King's love for Gentiles and Jews.
He died, but he's risen. There is hope for mankind,
Through the deepest of darkness a new light will shine.
Hatred and death your day is now done
For hope, love and life the victory have won.

And this foolish King looks to me and to you
invites us to be part of this story too.
Will we, with his flame burning inside
Tell others of grace and hope that's alive.

Will we be fools for Christ, he invites us to choose
To give up our rights - we've nothing to lose -
Because we'll gain life in all of its glory
Taking our place in his everlasting story.

Through his words and his deeds his message rings through
that God's love is boundless for me and for you
Wherever we've strayed, whatever we've done,
there's always a way back to the arms of the Son.
Thanks to the events of that Sunday morning
There'll always be hope that a new day is dawning.
So, come let us celebrate Jesus the King
and hope that he makes us as foolish as him.

PART 6
Journeying in Hope

A Devotional for Holy Week and Easter Season

For a couple of years, I posted daily Tweet-length Bible passages accompanied by short reflections. Here are 28 daily readings and reflections for Holy Week and Easter. If you wish you could use this as a short devotional during this season.

Day 1 – Palm Sunday

When Jesus came near the Mount of Olives, the whole crowd of disciples began joyfully to praise God in loud voices for all the miracles they had seen:
'Blessed is the king who comes in the name of the Lord!'
'Peace in heaven and glory in the highest!'
(Luke 19:28-40)

Just imagine being in the crowd that day, welcoming the King and praising God for all the wonders they'd witnessed. Their praise echoed the angels' song as they heralded Jesus' birth - peace was coming to earth through King Jesus, who made it possible for us to be right with God.

Day 2 – Monday of Holy Week

A teacher of the law asked Jesus, "Of all the commandments, which is the most important?" Jesus replied, "The most important is this: 'Love the Lord your God with all your heart, soul, mind and strength.' The second is this: 'Love your neighbour as yourself.'"
(Mark 12:28-31)

After a series of questions designed to trap Jesus, he finally receives one that's genuine. Of all the laws, what matters most? Jesus' answer takes a moment to remember but a lifetime to live out. Love God with everything you are, and then love each other. May God help us to love.

Day 3 – Tuesday of Holy Week

"Leave her alone, said Jesus, "Why are you bothering her? She's done a beautiful thing to me. The poor you'll always have with you; help them any time you want. But you won't always have me. She did what she could. She anointed my body beforehand for burial."
(Mark 14:6-8)

In response to the disciples' outrage at the woman, Jesus defends her. She is, at that moment, God's gift of grace to him. How many people had done something to show their appreciation for him without expecting anything in response? What beautiful thing could you do for Jesus?

Day 4 – Wednesday of Holy Week

Jesus knew that the Father had put all things under his power, that he'd come from God and would return to God; so he got up and wrapped a towel around his waist. Then, he poured water into a basin and began to wash his disciples' feet.
(John 13:3-5)

This is the most offensive thing Jesus ever did, lowering himself to the status of a slave, cleaning mess off his followers' feet. No wonder Peter was so shocked; he couldn't bear to see his Lord stoop so low. And yet, this embodies the love Jesus want to see in his kingdom.

Day 5 – Maundy Thursday

Jesus took bread, gave thanks, broke it, and gave it to them, saying,
'This is my body given for you; do this to remember me.'
In the same way, after supper he took the cup, saying, 'This cup's the
new covenant in my blood, which is poured out for you.'
(Luke 22:19-20)

At the heart of our faith is this meal that Jesus gave us to remember the glorious truth that his body was broken and blood was poured out for us, to enable us to be forgiven and to establish a new relationship between us and God. May we never lose the wonder of his mercy.

Day 6 – Good Friday

At noon, darkness came over the whole land until three in the afternoon.
And at three in the afternoon Jesus cried out in a loud voice, "Eloi,
Eloi, lema sabachthani?" (which means "My God, my God, why have
you forsaken me?").
(Mark 15:33-34)

Jesus was torn apart by the burden of humanity's sins as much as the nails and the cross. He endured the agony of separation from his Heavenly Father and bore our sins so that we might be free of them and know the reality that absolutely nothing can separate us from God's love.

Day 7 – Holy Saturday

When he had received the drink, Jesus said, "It is finished." With that,
he bowed his head and gave up his spirit.
(John 19:30)

It is finished.
Over now.
The evil they unleashed on you,
Whips and nails,
threats and curses,
Shall not hurt you any more.
You can rest now,
faithful servant.
Your battle's ended,
your work is done.
It is finished,
this all had purpose.
Night has fallen,
but the day will dawn.

Day 8 – Easter Sunday

They saw a young man dressed in a white robe sitting on the right side of
the tomb, and they were alarmed. "Don't be alarmed," he said. "You're
looking for Jesus the Nazarene, who was crucified. He has risen! He is
not here. See the place where they laid him."
(Mark 16:5-6)

The two women came to the tomb to anoint Jesus' body, the
last act of devotion they could give to their Lord. Instead,
they were the first witnesses of the world-changing news that
Jesus was alive. Because of the resurrection death and sin
have lost their grip and hope has dawned.

Day 9 – Easter Monday

*"Mary!" Jesus said. She cried out, "Teacher!" Jesus said, "Don't cling
to me. Go and tell my brothers, 'I'm ascending to my Father and your
Father, to my God and your God.'" Mary Magdalene found the
disciples and told them: "I've seen the Lord!"*
(John 20:16-18)

That one word changed everything. "Mary", said so tenderly
by the man she'd believed would never say her name again.
Hope flooded back - and then purpose: "Go, and tell my
brothers..." What a privilege, to be the first messenger of that
most incredible news - Jesus is alive!

Day 10 – Tuesday

*The men said to them, 'Why do you look for the living among the dead?
He's not here; he's risen! Remember what he told you in Galilee? "The
Son of Man must be delivered over to the hands of sinners, be crucified
and on the third day be raised again."'*
(Luke 24:5-7)

The disciples didn't expect Jesus to rise from the dead. Yet,
as the angels explained, this was always God's plan. St Paul
explains, "Christ died for our sins ... he was buried ... he was
raised on the third day according to the Scriptures"
(1Corinthians 15). Jesus died and rose again to save us.

Day 11 – Wednesday

Jesus himself stood among them and said to them, 'Peace be with you.' They were frightened, thinking they saw a ghost. He said to them, 'Why are you troubled? Why do you doubt what you see? Look at my hands and feet. It is I myself! Touch me and see.'
(Luke 24:36-39)

Jesus' risen presence speaks peace to our confusion and fright. Jesus' risen presence also gives us a hint of our destiny. Though our bodies will fail, God will give us new bodies that won't decay, fit for life in God's new creation. This is the hope he calls us to proclaim.

Day 12 – Thursday

Now, brothers and sisters, I want to remind you of the gospel I preached to you, which you received and on which you have taken your stand. By this gospel you are saved, if you hold firmly to the word I preached to you. Otherwise, you have believed in vain.
(1 Corinthians 15:1-2)

Christians are soft targets for ridicule, dismissed as weak and credulous. We're tempted to keep quiet as we feel embarrassed about our faith. Let's hold firm and continue to proclaim that Christ died for this broken world, but rose again, that he's the only hope for humanity.

Day 13 – Friday

If only for this life we have hope in Christ, we are of all people most to be pitied. But Christ has indeed been raised from the dead, the firstfruits of those who have fallen asleep. For as in Adam all die, so in Christ all will be made alive.
(1 Corinthians 15:19, 20, 22)

Recently I've used part of my Easter sermon to teach the congregation why we can be confident that Jesus rose from the dead. Paul was no stranger to people dismissing this as a story; as he points out, if the resurrection didn't happen then Christianity is a total waste of time.

Day 14 – Saturday

"Where, O death, is your victory? Where, O death, is your sting?" The sting of death is sin, and the power of sin is the law. But thanks be to God! He gives us the victory through our Lord Jesus Christ.
(1 Corinthians 15:55-57)

Perhaps the biggest difference the resurrection makes is that it destroys fear, as Jesus has broken the power of death. As Martin Luther King said, "I'm happy tonight; I'm not worried about anything; I'm not fearing any man. Mine eyes have seen the glory of the coming of the Lord."

Day 15 – Sunday

"When Jesus was at the table with them, he took bread, gave thanks, broke it and began to give it to them. Then their eyes were opened and they recognized him, and he disappeared from their sight."
(Luke 24:30-31)

The resurrection means new hope. The two disciples were bereft and hopeless until Jesus joined them on the road and everything changed. Using the Scriptures, he showed how his suffering was part of God's plan; then he broke bread and hope rose again. May God open our eyes to hope.

Day 16 – Monday

They got up and returned at once to Jerusalem. There they found the Eleven and those with them, assembled together and saying, "It is true! The Lord has risen and has appeared to Simon."
(Luke 24:33-34)

The resurrection means a fresh start. Verse 34 is one of my favourite Bible verses. Peter had screwed up badly, denying Jesus. He deserved to be snubbed and discredited. Instead the risen Jesus met privately with him and he encountered grace. With Jesus there's always a way back.

Day 17 – Tuesday

Jesus said, "Put your finger here; see my hands. Put your hand into the wound in my side. Stop doubting & believe." Thomas exclaimed, "My Lord and my God!" Jesus told him, "You believe because you've seen me; blessed are those who believe without seeing me."
(John 20:27-29)

The resurrection means that Jesus accepts us fully, doubt and all. Thomas spent 3 years with Jesus, heard him speak about the resurrection, yet didn't believe the disciples. Jesus appeared again, just for him. Jesus meets us where we are but doesn't want to leave us there.

Day 18 – Wednesday

Jesus said to Simon Peter, "Simon son of John, do you love me more than these?" "Yes, Lord," he said, "you know that I love you." Jesus said, "Feed my lambs."
(John 21:15)

The resurrection means fresh purpose. Jesus not only forgave Peter for screwing up by denying him, he commissioned him to lead the Jesus movement after his ascension. For us this means no matter how much we've let him down, Jesus has a role for us to play in his Kingdom purposes.

Day 19 – Thursday

Praise be to the God and Father of our Lord Jesus Christ! In his great mercy he has given us new birth into a living hope through the resurrection of Jesus Christ from the dead, and into an inheritance that can never perish, spoil or fade.
(1 Peter 1:3-4)

The resurrection means that the best is yet to come. Whatever we go through in life - trials, challenges, setbacks and disappointments - is only temporary. This life is not all there is. Jesus has secured for us a future beyond our imagining. Nothing can take that away from us.

Day 20 – Friday

Abraham wasn't counted as righteous just for his benefit, but for ours too - God will also count us as righteous if we believe in him, who raised Jesus from the dead. He was delivered over to death for our sins and was raised to life for our justification.
(Romans 4:23-25)

The resurrection means forgiveness. Our sins were nailed to the cross as the sinless one became sin for us, paying the price for the bad things we've done. When he rose again, the charge-sheet against us was torn up, it's forgotten; we're forgiven, made clean and purified.

Day 21 – Saturday

The death Jesus died, he died to sin once for all; but the life he lives, he lives to God. In the same way, count yourselves dead to sin but alive to God in Christ Jesus.
(Romans 6:10-11)

The resurrection means we are called to live holy lives. If Jesus died to take our sin away, why continue living a sinful lifestyle? Doing so cheapens grace, taking it for granted. Instead, we're called to strive for godliness, so that Jesus' light shines through us unhindered.

Day 22 – Sunday

But now that you have been set free from sin and have become slaves of God, the benefit you reap leads to holiness, and the result is eternal life. For the wages of sin is death, but the gift of God is eternal life in Christ Jesus our Lord.
(Romans 6:22-23)

The resurrection means that God can break us free from sinful habits that so often plague us, that we feel we'll never shake off. He not only clothes us with Jesus' perfection, but he works in our lives to make us more perfect. So, don't despair, he's not finished with you yet!

Day 23 – Monday

Give thanks to the Father who has qualified you to share in the saints' inheritance in the light. He delivered us from the power of darkness and transferred us to the kingdom of the Son he loves, in whom we have redemption, the forgiveness of sins.
(Colossians 1:12-14)

The resurrection means we become citizens of a different kingdom. Jesus has brought us from darkness into light. He has saved and forgiven us. Our calling is to be those who live with gratitude for all Jesus has done for us - expressing that verbally and in the way we live.

Day 24 – Tuesday

The dead in Christ will rise first. After that, we who are still alive and are left will be caught up together with them in the clouds to meet the Lord in the air. And so we will be with the Lord forever. Therefore encourage one another with these words.
(1 Thessalonians 4:16-18)

The resurrection means we are called to be people of hope. It's so easy to despair when we hear the latest news, and to wonder if there's any hope for humanity. But Jesus hasn't given up on us, so we mustn't either. We're called to keep looking up and to encourage each other.

Day 25 – Wednesday

In all things God works for the good of those who love him, who have been called according to his purpose. For those God foreknew he also predestined to be conformed to the image of his Son, that he might be the firstborn among many brothers and sisters.
(Romans 8:28-29)

The resurrection means that there's no situation in our lives so bleak or challenging that it's beyond God's power to bring hope, restoration and healing. Nothing is wasted in God's economy. In all things God's creative power is at work in our lives to make us more like Jesus.

Day 26 – Thursday

Say among the nations, "The Lord reigns." The world is firmly established, it cannot be moved; he will judge the peoples with equity.
(Psalm 96:10)

The resurrection means there is hope for the earth, because the Lord is King. Though rulers make bold claims and commit heinous deeds that seemingly go unpunished, in the end justice will triumph. In the meantime, God calls us not to despair, but to pray and work for that justice.

Day 27 – Friday

*The Lord has made his salvation known and revealed his righteousness
to the nations. He has remembered his love and his faithfulness to Israel;
all the ends of the earth have seen the salvation of our God.*
(Psalm 98:2-3)

The resurrection means that God keeps his promises. Here
and elsewhere the Scriptures prophesied that God would
bring about salvation for the world. Hundreds of years later
he did this through Jesus. If you're clinging to a promise
from God then hold on, because he is faithful.

Day 28 – Saturday

*Give thanks to the Lord, proclaim his name; make known his deeds
among the peoples. Sing praise to him; tell of all his wonderful acts.
Glory in his holy name; let the hearts of those who seek the Lord rejoice.
Seek the Lord and his strength continually.*
(Psalm 105:1-4)

The resurrection demands a response. Firstly, give thanks for
all God's done; secondly, testify to his work in our lives and
through the risen Jesus; thirdly, seek him and his will for us.
If he's saved us, we belong to him; he has the right to guide
what we do with our new life.

Appendix One – "Father, forgive" – Outline of a Devotional Service (based on the Gospel of Mark)

Opening Prayer

Hymn: My song is love unknown

Reading: Mark 14:43-52

Reflection: Judas Iscariot "The guilt won't let me go"

Hymn: Come and see

Reading: Mark 14:53-72

Reflection: Peter – "I let him down"

Reading: Mark 15:1- 15

Reflection: Barabbas – "He took my place"

Hymn: My Lord, what love is this

Reading: Mark 15:16-47

Reflection: Peter – A brand new start

Response

Hymn: And can it be

Prayer/blessing

Appendix Two – The Scandal of Grace – Outline of a Devotional Service (based on the Gospel of Luke)

<u>Opening Prayer</u>

<u>Hymn: Here is love vast as the ocean</u>

<u>Reading: Luke 22:47-62 (4 mins)</u>

<u>Reflection: Peter – "I let him down" (4 mins)</u>

<u>Silent Confession</u>

<u>Hymn: Come and see</u>

<u>Reading: Luke 22:63 – 23:25</u>

<u>Reflection: Barabbas – "He took my place"</u>

<u>Hymn: My Lord, what love is this</u>

<u>Reading: Luke 23:26-43</u>

<u>Reflection: A thief in paradise</u>

<u>Hymn: When I survey</u>

<u>Reading: Luke 23:44-49</u>

<u>Reflection: The centurion</u>

<u>Reading: Luke 23:50-56</u>

Andy March

Reflection: Joseph of Arimathea – "Out of the Shadows"

Hymn: My song is love unknown (5 mins)

Prayer/blessing

Appendix Three – Faith, hope, and courage – Outline of a Devotional Service (based on the Gospel of John)

<u>Opening Prayer</u>

<u>Hymn: There is a green hill far away</u>

<u>Reading: John 18:28-40</u>

<u>Reflection: Pontius Pilate – The blame game (1)</u>

<u>Reading: John 19:1-16</u>

<u>Reflection: Pontius Pilate – The blame game (2)</u>

<u>Response</u>

<u>Hymn: Come and see</u>

<u>Reading: John 19:16-27</u>

<u>Reflection: Mary – sunshine and shadows</u>

<u>Response</u>

<u>Hymn: My song is love unknown</u>

<u>Reading: John 19:28-42</u>

<u>Reflection: Nicodemus – No longer afraid</u>

<u>Response</u>

<u>Hymn: When I survey</u>

<u>Prayer/blessing</u>

<u>Collect</u>
Eternal God, in the cross of Jesus
we see the cost of our sin and the depth of your love:
in humble hope and fear may we place at his feet
all that we have and all that we are,
through Jesus Christ our Lord. Amen.[*]

---

[*] From Archbishop's Council, *Common Worship: Services and Prayers for the Church of England*, Church House Publishing (2000)

Printed in Great Britain
by Amazon